Kojo,

The Premium Leader

Leadership Attributes and Strategies for Today's Volatile World

You are an inspiration
to all of us -

DAYO OLOMU

"VUCA world, 4th Industrial Revolution and the COVID-19 pandemic climate, all require a premium leader."
Dayo Olomu

Also, by Dayo Olomu

- *4 Indispensable Strategies for Success*
- *My 50 Greatest Lessons in Life and Winning Principles for Success*
- *You Got the Power*

THE PREMIUM LEADER: Leadership Attributes and Strategies for Today's Volatile World

Copyright © 2021 Dayo Olomu

Dayo Olomu asserts the moral right to be identified as the author of this book under the Copyright, Designs and Patent Act 1988.

ISBN: 978-0-9550679-5-2

A CIP catalogue record for this title is available from the British Library

Dayo Olomu Publishing

Office: +44 (0) 871218773

Mobile: +44 (0) 7956065608 (UK)   +234 (0) 8039736164 (Nigeria)

E-Mail: info@dayoolomu.com and iconicddo@gmail.com

Dedication

────────────

I dedicate the book to all leaders and aspiring leaders, who want to make a positive difference in the world, and who would like to leave a legacy behind as a leader.

THE PREMIUM LEADER: Leadership Attributes
and Strategies for Today's Volatile World

Acknowledgements

I would like to acknowledge all those who made this book possible.

I want to start by thanking the Almighty God, my maker, for giving me the ability and divine inspiration to write this book. With you Lord, ALL things are, indeed possible. All that I am and hope to be, I owe it to you. I can do all things through Christ who strengthens me.

To my lovely wife, Goddess, and my beautiful children; thank you all for loving me, supporting, encouraging, and believing in me. It wouldn't have been possible to write this book without all of you by my side. I am eternally grateful. I love you all.

Special thanks to Dr. Yomi Garnett who worked on the first manuscript in 2016 and to Pastor Ladi Ayodeji who also worked on the manuscript in 2020.

Also, thanks to Prof John Adair, the first British professor of leadership who sowed the seed of writing the book in me, when I had lunch with him on my 48th birthday in 2013.

Finally, to my editor, Segun Martins Fajemisin, who turned the manuscript into a book.

THE PREMIUM LEADER: Leadership Attributes
and Strategies for Today's Volatile World

Contents

Dedication i
Acknowledgement iii
Foreword 1
Preface 3

PART 1 - Perspectives on Leadership
Chapter 1 11
An overview of leadership

Chapter 2 29
The concept of VUCA and the 4th Industrial Revolution

PART 2– Premium Leadership: The Seven Attributes to Lead & Thrive in a Digitally Transformed VUCA World

Chapter 3 57
Awareness (Attribute 1)

Chapter 4 79
Anticipation (Attribute 2)

Chapter 5 97
Adaptability (Attribute 3)

Chapter 6 131
Accountability (Attribute 4)

Chapter 7 .... **147**
Inspirational (Attribute 5)

Chapter 8.. **195**
Resilience – Overturning adversity (Attribute 6)

Chapter 9.. **213**
Audacity (Attribute 7)

Chapter 10 .... **225**
Conclusion

Chapter 11 .... **233**
Last Words

Chapter 12 .... **239**
A Message about Africa

APPENDICES
• How to Fast-Track Your Leadership Development
  (Top 12 Tips) 249
• 50 Leadership Quotes that I most admire 269
• References and Further Readings 275
• Profile of Dayo Olomu 279
• Testimonials/Accolades.. 285
• Epilogue 289

Foreword

―――――――――

Most institutions and nations have democratically elected leaders. This means we use popularity as a proxy for ability but history has taught us that leadership is populism, yet the practice continues. A cursory analysis of leadership failure exposes this misconception and this needs to be rectified through education and reorientation. This book sets out how you can acquire the skills needed for successful leadership. Since the world has been in turmoil for decades due primarily to the failure of leadership, this book is a welcome addition in addressing this serious issue.

All the tell-tale signs are there – economic dysfunction in several countries, which has given birth to violent protests, corruption, terrorism, wars, street crimes, racial unrests, and general political instability.

Dayo Olomu's latest book, *The Premium Leader*, hits the bull's eye with a comprehensive analysis of a global "virus" of leadership deficit that is plaguing all nations.

He provides a diverse and profound elixir to the intriguing issues that have intrigued scholars for ages, regarding how to manage a world, riven by disease pandemic, poverty, inequality, trade disputes, climate change and crime.

This book provides an overview of leadership, and addresses the concept of VUCA and the 4th Industrial Revolution. But the core of the book, is its strength in the listing of a Premium leader's attributes.

These attributes – *Awareness, Anticipation, Adaptability, Accountability, Inspirational, Resilience* and *Audacity* are treated in various chapters.

But the clincher for me, is the author's ability to paint the portrait of a real leader (The Premium Leader) that we need to run the world in troubled times. Olomu is able to demonstrate that, anyone can steady the ship when the sea is calm, but you need a special kind of captain to steer the ship in turbulent waters.

Such leaders must be highly inspiring, bold, competent and able to think outside the box. In addition, the Premium leader must have the requisite skills and strategies to deal with unpredictable problems as they arise.

For these reasons, I commend this book which has all the hallmarks of a bestseller, to every leader.

Professor Chris Imafidon
Multi Guinness World record holder;
Internationally acclaimed Adviser to Monarchs, Presidents, Governments and Corporate Leaders;
Chair, ExcellenceinEducation.org.uk Program
& Mentor to New York Times bestselling authors

Preface

―――――――――

The date was 3 August 2016. The place was Dubai, in the United Arab Emirates. I had planned my day very well in advance. When I woke up in the morning, I said my prayers, meditated and went to the gym.

After my speaking engagement on "Transformational Leadership" at a leadership conference, I went on a 2-hour sea cruise around the Palm Jumeirah to Burj Al Arab, Dubai Marina and 'The World' Islands before catching my 1.00 am flight back to London.

On getting back to the hotel, I went to my room and packed my suitcase. I went to the reception and ordered a taxi to take me to the airport. There and then, I was told that there was a plane crash at the Dubai International Airport in the morning. That was the first plane crash of the Emirates Airline. It shocked me. I later left for the airport. When I arrived, I was told that there is a six-hour delay. That threw all my plans out of the window. Welcome to a world riddled with complexities, or more aptly, the VUCA World! That's the acronym for volatile, uncertain, complex and ambiguous.

We live in a *Volatile, Uncertain, Complex* and *Ambiguous* world today. The surprise results in the UK referendum on Brexit, the US, French, UK and Austria general elections, the crisis in the Korean Peninsula and the political uncertainty in the key oil-producing countries of the Middle East and South Korea are good examples of this. What you think you will do tomorrow may not be the reality when that tomorrow comes. Klaus Schwab, author of *The Fourth Industrial Revolution,* said, "We stand on the brink of a technological revolution that will alter the way we live, work, and relate to one another". According to Klaus Schwab, "we are now in the Fourth Industrial Revolution". He added that, it's so complex and fast-moving that it demands a new type of leadership that "empowers all citizens and organisation to innovate, invest and deliver value in a context of mutual accountability and collaboration."

The question is, what do we do with all that is happening in the world today because that is the reality? "Everything rises and falls on leadership," says Dr. John C Maxwell, the American author, speaker, and pastor who has written many books, primarily focusing on leadership. But knowing how to lead is only half the battle. In this 21st century, we must approach leadership from another perspective.

As most people are painfully aware, few leaders–in all spheres could foresee the chain of events in 2008 that plunged the world into recession. Of those who predicted the meltdown, only few could draw a strategy to mitigate relevant risks such as the recent sharp drop in crude oil prices. "What is the way forward for organisations to maintain growth and manage risks in this VUCA world, which is a veritable minefield of disruptive and potentially discontinuous political, social, economic, and business changes that would exasperate even the most competent and alert CEOs, without rearming themselves with new behaviour and techniques, both at individual and corporate levels?" **(Abidi and Joshi, 2015).** We must fit our leadership style for a purpose.

The VUCA World and the Fourth Industrial Revolution offer tremendous opportunities to those who are prepared and who can expect. The nineteenth-century British banker and financier,

Nathan Rothschild, noted that it makes great fortunes when cannon balls fall in the harbour, not when violins play in the ballroom. Rothschild understood that the more unpredictable the environment, the greater the opportunity–if you have the leadership skills to capitalise on. **(Abidi and Joshi, ibid).**

These are challenging times. We are in a VUCA World–a world that is characterised by volatility, uncertainty, complexity and ambiguity. We know that the skills and abilities that got us here cannot take us to the future. Traditional leadership abilities won't be enough. Leaders need to up their game. *"We are in a new world, using old tools"* – according to Thomas Friedman, in the book, *The World Is Flat.*

This powerful book explores the new abilities and skills to lead and thrive in the current climate of VUCA World and the Fourth Industrial Revolution. In this book, I will share Strategic Insights and Solution (SIS) that will propel you to become an outstanding leader, who can lead and thrive in the prevailing situation.

The objective of this book is to introduce readers and leaders to the abilities you need to lead and thrive in the Volatile, Uncertain, Complex and Ambiguous (VUCA) World and the Fourth Industrial Revolution.

With the advent of COVID – 19, VUCA clearly shows its relevance and is the core principle to apply if leaders are to steer their nations out of the dysfunction this pandemic has caused worldwide. Institutions and nation-states are now facing inevitable and even predictable change. But they seem to lack the leadership, flexibility and imagination to adapt. Not that some of their current leaders don't recognise what's happening. It's just that the speed of change is merely overwhelming for them. This is the era of a new world of business, or as it is commonly quoted, "the new normal."

In this new environment, we are inexorably moving from a world of problems to a world of dilemmas. Solving problems requires speed, analysis, and elimination of uncertainty. Difficulties demand patience, sense-making, and engagement with uncertainty. Dilemmas require a different orientation, decision process, and a set of skills because dilemmas span disciplines and frustrate efforts to find workable solutions quickly enough.

Part of the problem is that too many corporate managers and leaders believe that the past continues to be an accurate predictor of the future. They continue to repeat and tweak the past to remain competitive. But, depending on past strategy does not ensure sustainability, and in fact, it might hasten an organisation's demise. Relying on the past might probably work when change is gradual, and innovation is incremental. But during disruptive and turbulent times, the required responses to change are not evolutionary but revolutionary.

In 'The World Is Flat,' Thomas Friedman notes that the rate of change today differs from what obtained in the past. *"Whenever civilization has gone through one of these disruptive, dislocating technical revolutions – like Gutenberg's introduction of the printing press, the world has changed in profound ways,"* he writes. *"But there is something different about the flattening of the world that will be qualitatively different from other such profound changes: the speed and breadth with which it is taking hold…. This flattening process is happening at warp speed and directly or indirectly touching a lot more people on the planet at once. The faster and broader this transition to a new era, the more likely it is the potential of disruption."*

The new environment will require every organisation to change its focus and methods of leadership development.

But the current clime, as Friedman notes, is taxing even the most able of leaders who may find their skills growing obsolete as quickly as their organisations change in this unstable, unpredictable landscape. We now require leadership agility and adaptability as is if organisations are to succeed in this VUCA world. Organisations today must change their business models, and their leadership skills, to become "adaptive firms." Now's VUCA business environment requires leaders to possess more complex and adaptive thinking abilities. These skills and abilities are a far cry from the more function-specific skills and abilities leaders needed in the past to succeed. Human resource and talent management professionals must refocus their leadership development efforts to hone these more strategic, complex, critical-thinking skills.

According to a research by Oxford Leadership: "*In the last 60 years, the average lifespan of a large organisation has dropped from 60 to just 18 years.*" The Harvard Business Review also reports that: "*the percentage of companies falling out of the top three rankings in their industry increased from two percent in 1960 to 14 percent in 2008.*"

What do we need?

We need agile learners. Rapidly changing context is like a treadmill that compels leaders to learn continuously in a self-directed mode. Leaders must be always curious and carry a "beginner's mind," which is also willing to give up on familiar approaches in an unlearning process. Leaders need meta-cognition and awareness of the bigger picture. When thrown into unfamiliar situations, leaders need to learn from those experiences.

We need to network and collaborate. To make any sense of the changing trends, practices and expectations, leaders in today's world need to work relentlessly within and outside the organisation. A social mindset enables leaders to create, engage with and nurture purposeful business and social networks through social media and in-person communication.

I have divided this book into 2 parts

Part I (Perspectives on leadership) covers the definition of leadership with particular emphasis on Authentic Transformational Leadership. This part also explores the meaning of VUCA and the Fourth Industrial Revolution.

Part 2 (The Seven Powerful Must-Have New Attributes to Lead & Thrive in a Digitally Transformed VUCA World) defines the qualities, skills, and behavioural attributes essential for leading and staying ahead in today's world. Essentially in this section, I have borrowed extensively from my 16 years' experience as a leader and proven empirical illustrations from acclaimed authors and thinkers on leadership. They are the relatable experiences and pointers that the average reader can utilise for a better understanding and reaching out in practical terms to becoming a functional leader in a VUCA world.

PART 1

(Perspectives on leadership)

Chapter 1

An Overview of Leadership

Core Leadership Theories

Leadership is probably the most frequently studied topic in the organisational sciences. Thousands of leadership studies have been published, and thousands of pages on leadership have been written in academic books and journals (Luthan, 2005). There are four core leadership theories that provide the backbone of the current understanding of leadership. First, the trait theories argue that effective leaders share several common personality characteristics or traits. Early trait theories said that leadership is an innate, instinctive quality that individuals have. None of these traits, nor any specific combination of them, guarantee success as a leader. Trait theories do, however, aid in identifying features and qualities such as integrity, empathy, and assertiveness that are helpful when leading others.

The second of the core leadership theories are behavioural theories. These theories focus on how leaders behave. In the 1930s, Kurt Lewin developed a framework based on a leader's behaviour. He argued that there are three types of leaders, specifically, the *autocratic*, *democratic*, and *laissez-faire* leader. Autocratic leaders decide without consulting their teams. I consider this style of leadership appropriate when decisions need to be made quickly, when there is no need for input and when team agreement is unnecessary for a successful outcome.

Democratic leaders allow the team to provide input before deciding, although information can vary from leader to leader. This style is outstanding when the team agreement matters. Laissez-faire leaders do not interfere and allow people within the team to make many decisions. This, however, can be difficult when there are various perspectives and ideas.

The third of the core leadership theories is the contingency or situational approach. A fundamental component of the contingency leader is that the organisation or workgroup affects the extent to which given leader traits and behaviours will be effective. Introduced in 1967, Fiedler's contingency theory was the first to specify how situational factors interact with leader traits and behaviour, to influence leadership effectiveness (Fiedler, 1967).

Contingency theories gained prominence in the late 1960s and 1970s. Four well-known contingency theories are Fiedler's contingency theory, path-goal theory, the Vroom-Yetton-Jago decision-making model of leadership, and the situational leadership theory.

The fourth of the core leadership theories is the power and influence theories. These theories focus on the source of the leader's power and are based on the different ways that leaders use power and influence to get things done. One of the best-known of these theories is French and Ravens' Five Forms of Power. This model highlights three types of positional power—legitimate, reward, coercive—and two sources of personal power—expert and referent. The model suggests that using their power is most effective when coupled with expertise as a legitimate source of their ability.

Another source of power and influence is transactional leadership. This approach assumes that people do things for reward and no other reason. Contrasting the transactional leadership style is the transformational leadership style. Transformational leaders show integrity and know-how to develop a robust and inspiring vision of the future. They motivate people to achieve this vision and manage their delivery. The transformational leader is most closely linked to the concept of self-leadership.

WHAT IS LEADERSHIP?

There is an indisputable mystery to leadership. To be considered a good or great leader, you are expected to be a Barack Obama, Bill Clinton, Hillary Clinton, Tony Blair, Angela Merkel, Genghis Khan, Winston Churchill, Joan of Arc, Martin Luther King, Benazir Bhutto, Nelson Mandela, Niccolò Machiavelli, Steve Jobs, Estee Lauder, Aliko Dangote, Jacinda Ardern, Napolean Bonaparte and Mahatma Gandhi, all rolled into one. Quite a few individuals feel comfortable calling themselves an excellent or great leader, and the rest of us think wholly inadequate, when measured against their standard. But the sphere of leadership goes beyond the political arena; it covers every facet of human life, as we would see later in the subsequent chapters of this book.

The mystery of leadership becomes more profound when an attempt is made to define a good or great leader.

There are many ways to finish the sentence, "Leadership is
...."

We all seem to recognise a good or great leader anytime we
encounter one. Yet, no leader appears capable of conforming to a
single template of characterisation.

As Stogdill (1974, p. 7) pointed out in a review of leadership
research, there are almost as many definitions of leadership as there
are people who have tried to define it. It is much like the words
democracy, love, and peace. Although each of us intuitively knows
what we mean by such terms, the words can have different
meanings for different people.

After decades of dissonance, leadership scholars agree on one
thing: They can't come up with a standard definition for leadership.

In the search for the holy grail of leadership, specific facts will
become incontrovertible:

- Everyone can be a leader.

- You don't need a title to be a leader.

- All leaders do certain things uncommonly well. This may not
  guarantee success, but it makes success more likely.

- You can learn to be a leader in your mould. You do not have to
  be a Mandela, Angela Merkel or Obama. You must be the best
  of who you already are; you must wake up your highest
  potential and believe in yourself.

Despite the multitude of ways in which leadership has been
conceptualised, the following components can be identified as
central to the phenomenon: (a) Leadership is a process, (b)
leadership involves influence, (c) leadership involves inspiration
(d) leadership occurs in groups, (e) leadership involves common
goals, and (f) leadership involves taking action. Based on these
components, we use the following definition of leadership in this
book:

"Leadership is a process whereby an individual sees, inspires and influences a group of individuals to turn their vision into action and achieve a common goal

– Dayo Olomu

Leadership is not necessarily related to seniority. It is not about position. Put in its simplest terms, it is about 'what you do' and 'how you behave.' Therefore, specific facts become clear:

- The person at the top of the organisation is in a leadership position, but may not be leading. He may merely be a cautious steward.

- Leaders can exist at all levels of an organisation.

- Leaders need followers. You may surpass Einstein in brilliance, but if no one is following you, you are not a leader.

- Circumstances may throw up a leadership challenge.

The skills and behaviours of effective leaders

- Many leaders lack management skills. Being proficient at memo-writing, presentations, accounting methods, strategy and even technical know-how, are useful, but ~~indispensable~~ **dispensable**.

- Intelligence would appear to be low on the priority list for effective leadership. Most business or political leaders are not necessarily the brightest or the most competent or the most skilled in their areas. Gates, Branson, Buffet and Abramovich do not have MBAs, and Churchill did not even go to university. This means you don't also need formal qualifications to be an effective leader.

While you may not need formal education to be a leader, you

need native intelligence. This is a common denomination in all leadership positions. Also, emotional interest is a basic tool of leadership today because it aids quick reaction to issues.

The contemporary leader must have a total dislike for the status quo, especially when the status quo translates to complacency, perceived, yet impractical boundaries and barriers, and a pervasive fear of failure. He must not only have profound compassion for people but also deep compassion for change, which compels him to search for or create the path toward a solution.

Compassion is one of the purest forms of the expression of love. Empathy is a commonly used word, and most people are understandably inclined to equate it with kindness. However, its meaning and application goes far beyond mere understanding. Its expression is a true reflection of the potential bigness of the human heart. It involves the willingness to do four things. Put yourself in someone else's shoes, take the focus off yourself, imagine what it's like to be in someone else's predicament, and then feel love for that person. Compassion is a profoundly silent and tender feeling which manifests as a constantly self-relinquishing demeanour. It elevates one above a self-centred existence, enabling one to live in the hearts of others and to think and feel with them. Human agony demands tenderness and help. Compassion feels that agony and eases it.

I feel compelled to commend all the people who find themselves in a classic setting of compassion. Countless individuals have enjoyed the excellent mentoring and coaching of such people. On their behalf, I express a sincere and profound appreciation for the superb work they are doing in helping as many people as humanly possible, to reach their full potential, to lead lives filled with genuine, spirit-filled purpose and passion. In the same breath, I hail and commend their selflessness, and their compassion for the powerless; the needy; the defenceless; the oppressed, and those with limited opportunities in a world that can be harsh, brittle and brutal.

Without doubt, in striving to spiritually, morally and economically empower others, these people are also encouraging them to get hold of their dreams and live their lives anew.

Each of us fulfilled a unique purpose, and the divine has manifested in us in human form, physical form if you like, to achieve this definite purpose. In living true to our own unique and particular purpose, we are manifesting an authentic nobility of spirit that celebrates all that is great about humanity.

Genuine leadership is anchored on connectivity of empathy and the ability to meet basic needs of the moment. Without this, leadership fails ab initio at the start, because inertia sets in leading to revolt of followers.

History and posterity will judge the compassionate leaders of this world most creditably for this generous contribution to the continued evolution of the human condition.

A leader in this century has a clear picture of an ambitious goal and a good cause. He can see what the desired end should be. This vision is indelibly etched on his heart and provides the impetus that drives him and enables him to drive his team.

But what, in real terms, is visionary leadership?

Vision is the ultimate consequence of the creative imagination. Vision has proved to be the fundamental emotive force that drives everything else in a leader's life. It is also, without an iota of doubt, the most potent motive for a leader's actions. Vision is the crucial ability to see beyond one's present reality. Vision eventually becomes one's compelling propensity to create, ultimately making vision one's innovative competence to invent what does not yet exist. Vision is the insight to transform, in the present moment, into the future form. Vision has gloriously given leaders the capacity to live out of their imagination, rather than out of their memories, allowing them not only to exist in the present moment but beyond their current reality. Of even greater significance, vision, more than any other factor, will invariably affect the choices the leader has to make.

Vision is the leader's mission ~~on~~ **in** pictures. A painter must first see the picture in his mind's eye, before he can paint it. So, it is with a leader. No leader succeeds without a clear vision. It is what stirs action and inspires followership.

Remarkably, vision also dictates, to a significant degree, the way a leader spends his time. This is the reason most leaders have the wholesome habit of always telling themselves that it hardly matters that they are doing so much, if what they are doing is not what matters most. It is also the reason, at any point in time, they pause to always ask this question:

"What is the most valuable use of my time at this instant?"

The contemporary leader draws upon all the charisma and persuasive power he possesses to share his vision, to raise and inspire a team. This empowers him with the resources and tools he needs to make impactful leadership a viable possibility. Practical communication skills are fundamental to success in many aspects of life. Virtually every human interaction requires strong communication skills, and people with improved communication skills usually enjoy better interpersonal relationships with friends and family. Effective communication is a critical interpersonal skill, and by learning how we can improve our conversation; we reap valuable benefits. Since communication is a two-way process, improving communication involves both how we send and receive messages.

Indubitably convinced of the possibilities and potentials of their dreams, leaders refuse to back down or be discouraged by the challenges that are inevitably thrown on their path. Instead, they maintain a positive and unrelenting attitude as they seek to drive change, and their capacity for converting obstacles into tools which they used to benefit them is legendary.

Your quintessential leader heroically combines an infectious charisma with sound character and excellent human relations, which all jointly invoke a sense of commitment, loyalty and respect from team members. His high sense of integrity breeds mutual trust among the team, and this increases effectiveness, as team members learn to possess individualistic ownership of the vision, and are prepared to run together with it, even at high personal cost. In its purest essence, this is synergy at play. Synergy is one of the essential concepts in productivity and personal development, and we consider it as being two or more people working together to achieve more than they could alone.

The word synergy comes from the Greek word 'synergia' which means working together. Therefore, synergy is the interaction of two or more agents or forces so that their combined effect is greater than the sum of their results. It has also been said that the power of synergy is exponential, as it doesn't work through addition, but through multiplication. In organisational behaviour, since a cohesive group is more than the sum of its parts, synergy is the ability of a group to outperform even its best individual member.

Leaders are humble enough to admit errors when they occur, to consider the views of other team members responsible, and to share their success and the legacy with them. The leader humbly refuses to take all the glory for his accomplishments and insists on giving everyone the grace and opportunity to share, not only in the story behind the glory, but also the glory after the story.

It requires a great deal of humility for cultivating healthy interpersonal relationships. One of the greatest of human failings is a lack of humility. A true leader brings genuine insight and understanding to his interpersonal relationships. Human inter-relationship is generally regarded as being very complex, yet it is simple, and the reason most people do not appreciate others is principally because of a lack of humility. No one crosses our path by accident. Every human being we must relate with, no matter how difficult, almost invariably has something valuable to teach us. It is easy to love someone who is sweet-nature and agreeable. Still, it takes monumental effort to display the same affection to a positively obnoxious individual. However, it is this person, one who disturbs our state of peace, which lets us know just how much work we genuinely must do on ourselves.

The greatest challenge of real leadership is the imperative of managing those who'd inevitably oppose the leader, no matter how well he leads. A leader must learn to cope with the loyal and the disloyal.

The leader is one who possesses a giant heart. He has come to the liberating understanding that altruism is a significant part of the quest for authentic fulfilment in life. The sages, for millennia, have always proclaimed that the real essence of life lies, in giving and that the hand of the giver will always be on top. It is an indisputable fact that, regardless of what you offer, a giver will never suffer lack. This shares a perfect analogy with the sharing of knowledge and the encouragement of others to learn. When you share your wealth of experience with others, life takes on a new sense of purpose for you and imbues you with a genuine feeling of satisfaction. This means, in its most straightforward connotation, that true fulfilment comes from impacting on lives. I am of the sincere conviction that nature commends us when we reach out to others, for aren't we all poor and less privileged in some respect or the other? Compassion in a leader's heart opens his eyes to the needs of the world around him. It affords him a fresh vision that becomes the propelling force that drives him to meddle and gets involved, not only in projects but in the lives of people.

It is altogether instructive to note that history is beautified with the experiences of meddling leaders, some of whom were noted for their impact in the civil right movements and the eradication of slavery. Slave trading along the coast of African nations did not end without the extraordinary sacrifices and selfless commitments of well-meaning leaders who had a compassionate heart driven by the crystal-clear vision of a free world, and a hard-earned dislike for the very concept of the dehumanising slave trade.

"We hold these truths to be self-evident: that all men are created equal; that their Creator endows them with certain unalienable rights; that among these are life, liberty and the pursuit of happiness", said Abraham Lincoln, the American President whose philosophy shaped the creation and implementation of the Emancipation Proclamation, and the 13th Amendment, which provided the inspiration and momentum that made black African slaves, free citizens, within the borders of the United States of America.

Another epic year worth remembering is 1833, which graced the abolition of the slave trade in Great Britain, a monumental effort rendered by implementing the Slavery Abolition Act passed by the House of Commons since 1807, a bill that cost William Wilberforce twenty-six years of toil, his health and eventually his life, three days after the law was fully enforced. The unacceptable circumstances of slavery forged the birth of these leaders because none of them started their careers to tackle those societal maladies we remember them for today. On reflecting on the lives of these purposeful leaders, one is reminded that the accurate measurement of a successful leader's impact is not the number of awards or accolades received, but the number of changed lives made possible by his or her unstinting dedication to a noble cause. Invariably, such selfless dedications are exact aftermath effects of individual experiences or causes that have shaped a leader's perspective on what real impact is and is not. This refined perspective equips a leader to discover his real legacy, which deviates from the noise of career success and the praises of men.

To be sure, not all leaders function in the klieg lights. Some of the greatest leaders are silent achievers who were not even recognised in their generations. That's why we have post-humous awards for those achievers whose contributions were not appreciated in their times.

As it is with creating any manner of change, the leader must first become a repository of that change, and from that fountain of change in him, liberally pour it out to the people closest to him.

Who Says You Can't Be a Leader?

At seven, they forced a young boy and his family out of their home. The boy had to work to support his family. At nine, his mother passed away. When he grew up, the young man was keen to go to law school but had no education.

At 22, he lost his job as a store clerk. At 23, he ran for the state legislature and lost. The same year, he went into business. It failed, leaving him with a debt that took him 17 years to pay. At 27, he had a nervous breakdown.

Two years later, he tried for the post of speaker in his state legislature. He lost. At 31, they defeated him in his attempt to become an elector. By 35, he had been defeated twice while running for congress. Finally, he secured a brief term in Congress, but at 39 he lost his re-election bid. At 41, his four-year-old son died. At 42, they rejected him as a prospective land officer. At 45, he ran for the Senate and lost. Two years later, he lost the vice-presidential nomination. At 49, he ran for senate and lost again. At 51, they elected him the President of the United States of America.

The man in question: Abraham Lincoln -   Author Unknown

Many of us are acquainted with the eloquent example of persistence in achieving victory. We read it, stop for a moment and then sigh and say, *"Wow! That's the real stuff leaders are made of."*

And in saying this, it's too comfortable from the rest of humanity and empowered by some mysterious quality that smoothens their path towards inevitable success. This is the view of leadership that many people have traditionally taken: that leaders are marked out for leadership early in their lives and that if you're not a leader, there's little that you can do to become one.

However, that's not now. The modern view is that through patience, persistence and hard work, you can gain the qualities of an effective leader. And that then, just as long as you make the effort needed, you can lead successfully.

Now, I ask you to take a moment of reflection. When I said, "That's the real stuff leaders are made of," just what stuff is this "stuff" we attributed to former U.S. President Lincoln? What is the "stuff" that made him prevail against all the odds to emerge as a great leader? It amounts to sheer determination and a desire to lead, doesn't it?

Are Leaders Born or Made?

"Like a musical instrument, genes do not determine what music is played. Gene defines the range of what can possibly be played." **– Warren Blank, Leadership Author**

"Sure, I want to be a leader, but I just don't have it in me!" This self-doubt holds many of us back from the leadership journey. I felt this when I was selected to lead some of my senior colleagues as the Founding President of Croydon Communicator Toastmasters 10 years ago. Ditch the doubt! Leadership is not the province of a select few; it is a learnable process. And if you genuinely want to, you can learn to become an effective leader.

The question isn't: "Are leaders born or made?"

That is like asking whether athletes are born or made. There is no single answer to the question, for we all know that it requires both inherent talent and hard training to build an exceptional athlete (and even athletes with few natural advantages can achieve tremendous things with hard practice and common sense).

The real question is "Can leadership be learned?"

And the answer to this question is a definite, definitive "YES." As I've said, the general perception is that leadership is a blend of unique, mysterious qualities. I take it for granted that either you are born with this elusive "right stuff" or not. This is a myth; there is nothing mysterious about most of the ingredients that go into the leadership cocktail. And most of these essential elements already lie within your reach.

Some leadership skills and behaviours are already present in you. You just have to learn to tap into them fully. Some of them may be foreign to you now, but with perseverance and application, you can learn to cultivate them.

Do you have to be a genius or have the charisma to become a leader?

Traits such as charisma and genius fall mainly in the "born" category and cannot be mastered thoroughly. But we usually attach far more importance to them than they deserve. No doubt such traits are major advantages, but if you have them and don't compliment them with other essential skills, they may not amount to much; and if you don't have them, but compensate for this deficit by strengthening other skills, you can still become a successful leader.

Management guru, Peter Drucker, uses former U.S President Harry Truman as a case study to underline this point. "Harry Truman did not have an ounce of charisma, yet he was among the most effective chief executives in US history."

Becoming an effective leader is not about becoming a master of all leadership skills. Instead, it is about recognising your strengths and weaknesses and then nurturing the former and overcome the latter.

Learn to recognise the tools and opportunities you have access to and then use them effectively to carry you forward in your leadership journey.

Kari H. Keating, Ph.D., a teaching associate at the University of Illinois at Urbana-Champaign, who studies leadership, co-authored an October 2014 study, which supported existing research that leaders are made, not born. Expanding on work by leadership researcher Bruce J. Avolio, which found that leadership ability is roughly 30% genetic and 70% learned, Keating and her colleagues found that the first step to becoming a more effective leader is to believe that you can be a leader.

What makes a leader?

A strange thing happened in March 1999. The stock price of a large, profitable computer company fell unexpectedly. "So, what!" you might say. Stock prices of computer companies are known to drop a lot. But this was March 1999, long before the Internet bubble burst. The stocks of all technology companies were on the up-and-up. Yet, the stock price of one of the most admired companies, the Dell Computer Company, fell.

We considered this strange because Dell was the exemplar of an innovative, high-performing technology company. It had invented the direct delivery model and executed it admirably. Its sales and profits were the envy of the industry. Yet, its stock price suddenly dropped sharply. Why?

An analyst with the Wall Street Journal explained the drop in stock price, but given the circumstances, perhaps the only plausible one. Dell biography has just been released. In reading it, investors realised that Michael Dell was just an ordinary guy, readily likened to "the fellow next door." This was no tough-talking Bill Gates, nor steely-eyed Jack Welch. Instead, Dell was just an easy-sounding, pleasant-looking guy: thus, the stock market had an unnerving realisation.

"What sort of leader was this? Could he be expected to lead a company through tough times?" Such thoughts seemed to cross the minds of investors in Dell, according to analyst.

Source: **Maira, Arun. Shaping the Future: Leadership through Communities of Aspiration in India and Beyond. (2002).**

The stereotypical view of a leader is the hero-leader, a guy who is bigger than life. However, years of leadership research show that this isn't necessarily a correct view. While the hero-leader is one leader, there are various other types of leaders. Today, after the failure of Enron and the bursting of the Dot-com bubble, different leaders occupy the centre stage.

One thing we must understand is that there is no one "correct" leadership style. The thing with leadership is that it is much better defined as a process than a list of qualities.

An effective leader is best defined as a person who:

- Identifies the right job that needs to be done

- Influences the right people, at the right time, to do the job

- Gets the job done right, in the right ways

For the qualities that help the leader achieve this process, there is no single shared view. While there are some traits and behaviours that seem to be associated with leaders, it is difficult to find out what matters most.

Summary

1   Who is a leader? Anyone who leads is a leader, regardless of the field in which they operate. Leaders are also born and made

2   Leadership spans every sphere

3   The concept of leadership has changed globally over the years to encompass all its various dimensions.

4   VUCA is a litmus test of successful leader.

Chapter 2

The concept of VUCA and the 4ᵗʰ Industrial Revolution

Origin of VUCA

The U.S. Army War College conceptualised the notion of VUCA to describe the more volatile, uncertain, complex, and ambiguous, multilateral world that resulted from the end of the Cold War. The acronym itself was not deployed until the late 1990s, and it was not until the terrorist attacks of September 11, 2001, that notion and acronym fused to become a reality. Strategic business leaders subsequently adopted VUCA to describe the chaotic, turbulent, and rapidly changing business environment that has become the "neo normal."

From all empirical indicators, the chaotic "new normal" in business is a genuine entity. The financial crisis of 2008-2009, for example, rendered many business models obsolete, as organisations throughout the world were plunged into turbulent environments like those faced by the military. Rapid changes irrevocably accompanied the explosion in technological developments like social media, while the world's population continued to grow simultaneously and age and global disasters disrupted lives, economies, and businesses.

Concept of VUCA

VUCA is an acronym developed by the U.S. military after the collapse of the Soviet Union, to describe a multipolar world: **V**olatile, **U**ncertain, **C**omplex and **A**mbiguous.

Volatility reflects the speed and turbulence of change. It means the nature, speed, volume, and magnitude of change is not in a predictable pattern. Volatility is turbulence, a phenomenon that is occurring more frequently than in the past. A study found that half of the most turbulent financial quarters during the past thirty years have occurred since 2002. The study also concluded that economic turbulence has increased in intensity and persists longer than in the past. Other drivers of turbulence in business today include digitisation, connectivity, trade liberalisation, global competition, and business model innovation.

Uncertainty means that outcomes, even from familiar actions, are becoming less and less predictable. But this is the lack of predictability in issues and events. These volatile times make it difficult for leaders to use past problems and incidents as predictors of future outcomes, making forecasting difficult and decision-making challenging.

Complexity shows the vastness of interdependencies in globally connected economies and societies. There are often many, and perhaps difficult-to-understand causes and mitigating factors, both inside and outside an organisation, involved in a problem.

This layer of complexity, added to the turbulence of change and the absence of past predictors, adds to the difficulty inherent in contemporary decision making. This also leads to confusion, which can cause *ambiguity*, the last letter in the VUCA acronym.

Ambiguity connotes the multitude of options, and the potential outcomes resulting from them. Where once we could count on the certainty and predictability of binary choices such as capitalism versus communism, democracy versus autocracy, choices and their attendant consequences are now far less clear than they used to be. Ambiguity is the lack of clarity about the meaning of an event. Put differently, the 'causes,' and the 'who, what, where, how, and why,' behind the things that are happening are now unclear and hard to find out. Put more elegantly, the ambiguity in the VUCA model is the inability to conceptualise threats and opportunities before they become lethal accurately. A symptom of organisational uncertainty is the frustration that results when compartmentalised accomplishments cannot add up to an overall or enduring success.

From regular triple-digits swings in the market to the rapid rise of often profit-free unicorns valued at US$1 billion or more, an exit of the United Kingdom from the European Union, the dissolution of the once-hopeful Arab Spring into the chaos of the Syrian civil war, and an increasing wave of turmoil, from Libya to Ukraine, this isn't just a VUCA world anymore, it's becoming ever more pervasively VUCA.

However, there is a ray of hope on the horizon. Although the leadership challenges in an increasingly VUCA world are significant, they are not impossible for those who will look beyond old thinking and approaches.

Here is some pragmatic guidance to help us craft a strategy.

VUCA doesn't mean that everything is unpredictable. If you step back to take a system-level view of the world, there are meta-phenomena with trend lines that are clear, even if not precisely delineated:

- *Urban concentrations*: most of the globe's population now live in cities, and this will continue to increase in the decades ahead. By mid-century, most of the top ten mega-cities in the world will be in the developing world. With urbanisation will come longer life expectancies, lower birth rates, and more excellent economic prospects.

- *Climate changes*: Even sceptics will have to accept that, while debate continues over the exact timing and consequences, the consensus that we are in the Anthropocene era, in which human activity is altering the climate is only strengthening. Sea levels will rise, extreme weather events will multiply, and water sources and agricultural production will be less reliable.

- *Demographic shifts*: Globally, the North and West are getting older, and the most significant concentrations of youth will be in the South and East. Tensions are likely to rise as the bulk of economic wealth, and opportunity remains beyond the reach of many people.

- *Technology advances*: We will be ever-more connected by devices that are smaller, faster, and less expensive. We can use each of these phenomena as a lens on your business and industry to make it easier to discern what may be coming.

VUCA and Leadership Development

This new VUCA environment is taxing even the most able of leaders who discover that their skills are growing obsolete as rapidly as their organisations are inexorably changing in this unstable, unpredictable landscape. We now require leadership agility and adaptability more now, if organisations are to succeed in this VUCA world. As Horney, Pasmore, and O'Shea, co-authors of 'Leadership Agility: A Business Imperative for a VUCA World' note, to succeed, *"leaders must make continuous shifts in people, process, technology, and structure. This requires flexibility and quickness in decision making."*

Organisations, now, must shift their business models, and their leadership skills, to become 'adaptive firms,' because 'adaptive firms' can adjust and learn better, faster, and more economically than their peers, giving them an 'adaptive advantage.'

A report by the Centre for Creative Leadership also notes that current's VUCA business environment requires leaders to possess more complex and adaptive thinking abilities. It also notes that the methods used to develop these new skill requirements, for instance, on-the-job training, coaching, and mentoring, have changed little. As a result, leaders are not growing fast enough or in the right ways to keep up with the "neo normal" for business.

Management professionals must position their organisations to succeed in today's turbulent business environment by developing agile leaders. Applying the VUCA model as a framework to re-tool leadership development models may enable Human Resource and Management professionals to identify and foster the leaders their organisations need now and.

A Case Study
Unilever

In 2010, Unilever, one of the world's largest consumer goods companies, pledged to double the size of their business in the next ten years while reducing its environmental footprint and increasing its social impact. Sustainability became a central component of its new business model. It was based on VUCA principles. When asked by Forbes why they changed their business model, Keith Reed, Unilever's chief marketing and communication officer, responded:

> "We look at the world through a lens which we call VUCA, which stands for 'Volatile, Unstable, Complex, and Ambiguous.' So, you can say, 'It's a very tough world,' or you can say, 'It's a world that's changing fast, and we can help consumers navigate through it.' Two-and-a-half billion more people will be added to the planet between now and 2050, of which 2 billion will be added in developing countries. The digital revolution, the shift in consumer spending, all this suggests that companies have to reinvent the way they do business."

To meet that VUCA challenge, Unilever has also changed its leadership development model.

BUT VUCA WAS ALWAYS THERE

The VUCA environment is not new.

When the Mongols suddenly arrived at the gates of Europe in the thirteenth century, it was VUCA, and the known world changed forever. VUCA brings with it both opportunities and failures. From the dawn of civilization, there have been spectacular failures ranging from the demise of the Persian Empire to the bankruptcy of Lehman Brothers, primarily because of the inability to read the impending changes. There have also been sterling cases of phoenix-like rising from failures such as Emperor Babur, who first lost his kingdom and rose again to lay the foundation of the Mughal Empire. (*Abidi and Joshi, 2015*).

The Story of Pan Am

Pan Am was a pioneer in air travel and a brand name second only to Coca Cola. Pan Am's founder, Juan Trippe, was the world's first airline tycoon, the imperial sky-god, his company the aviation pioneer that came to be known as America's Imperial Airlines.

First, to fly the Pacific, first across the Atlantic, first around the world, Pan Am was once one of the most glamorous and best-known global corporations. Its worldwide headquarters–the crown jewel–was on Manhattan's Park Avenue, The Pan Am Building, the world's largest corporate office building.

America's heavily regulated airline industry comprised two parts: the domestic airlines and the international airlines: Pan Am and TWA. The idea was simple: the domestic airlines delivered passengers to international gateways, where the international airlines picked them up and took them overseas. Pan Am enjoyed this arrangement. Until 1978, when the industry was deregulated. It was more comfortable for the domestic carriers to add international service than it was for Pan Am and TWA to build national networks of domestic flights to feed their global function. It was one of a series of setbacks for the proud pioneer. The expensive 747s arrived just as a recession hit and air travel slowed. Then the Arab oil embargo in 1973 and 1974 increased jet fuel prices, and after that came deregulation.

Pan Am was buffeted like a propeller plane in an updraft, handicapped not only by its lack of a domestic route system but also by an uninspiring succession of chief executives and top-heavy management. Labour unions also were slow to make concessions. *"Circumstances caused half of Pan Am's problem,"* a frustrated onetime financial advisor to the company says. *"The other half was caused by the culture, which seemed to make perfectly rational men think they were invulnerable once they walked through Pan Am's doors. The Pan Am of legend is long gone. It went bankrupt in 1991, and The Pan Am building was sold and is now called MetLife. A disruptive technology did not defeat it but by VUCA, changes in the business environment, primarily the deregulation of airlines, which called for agility that monolithic companies did not possess, something our own Air India is very familiar with. If Air India were a private airline, it would also have gone into oblivion a long time ago."* (Jon Marcus and Gretchen Voss, *'Air Apparent,'* **Boston Magazine**, February 2000).

The 4ᵗʰ Industrial Revolution

"The Fourth Industrial Revolution is the current and developing an environment in which disruptive technologies and trends such as the Internet of Things (IoT), robotics, virtual reality (VR) and artificial intelligence (AI) are changing the way we live and work.

The third industrial revolution, sometimes called the digital revolution, involved the development of computers and IT (information technology) since the middle of the 20th century. The Fourth Industrial Revolution is growing out of the third. Still, it is considered a new era rather than a continuation because of the explosiveness of its development and the disruptiveness of its technologies. According to Professor Klaus Schwab, Founder and Executive Chairman of the World Economic Forum and author of The Fourth Industrial Revolution, the new age is differentiated by the speed of technological breakthroughs, the pervasiveness of scope and the tremendous impact of new systems.

The first industrial revolution, in the 18th and 19th centuries, involved a change from mostly agrarian societies to greater industrialisation because of the steam engine and other technological developments. Electricity drove the next technological age, the second industrial revolution, and it involved an expansion of industries and mass production and technological advances." **(Ivy Wigmore, Feb 2020)**

In her first party conference speech as Prime Minister, Theresa May declared that it was "time to remember the good that government can do". Setting out a new approach to the role of the state, she rightly acknowledged that Whitehall doesn't have all the answers but should instead be a proactive "force for good". *(Julian Harris, Oct, 2016)*

That's undoubtedly the right approach for helping Britain lead the Fourth Industrial Revolution (4IR), as a new wave of technological breakthroughs is known. From advanced robotics, driverless cars and 3D printers to Amazon's delivery drones, internet-connected household devices and nanotechnology, these innovations are transforming the way we live and work. *(Alan Mak, Mar 2017)*

I was privileged to be one of the "influential audience from the worlds of entrepreneurship, technology, media and investment", invited by the Duke of York as a judge at the *Pitch@Palace Commonwealth* to showcase Entrepreneurs from Commonwealth countries as part of the activities of the members of the Royal Family during the Commonwealth Heads of Government Summit (CHOGM2018) in London.

Pitch@Palace allows entrepreneurs to meet the people who can help make their business dreams become a reality. *Pitch@Palace* guides help and connect entrepreneurs and early-stage businesses with potential supporters, including CEOs, influencers, angels, mentors and business partners.

Entrepreneurs are selected to take part in *Pitch@Palace* and are invited to attend a boot camp. They receive support and guidance on how to develop and hone their Pitch, and support with investment, introductions and strategic direction. They invite all the Entrepreneurs selected for Boot Camp to the final event at St. James's Palace and a selection of these businesses pitch directly to an influential audience from the worlds of entrepreneurship, technology, media and investment. The support does not end there. All the *Pitch@Palace* entrepreneurs, whether selected to pitch at St. James's Palace or not, join the growing alumni network of entrepreneurs and receive ongoing support.

After the event, they hosted us to cocktails by the Duke, where I got talking with business and political leaders from China. I asked them how China is preparing for the Fourth Industrial Revolution. I was shocked by what I was told. China is way ahead of many countries in terms of the use of artificial intelligence and robotics technology. I was told that they now have some automated factories staffed by robotics.

With global disruption creating new ways of creating value such as Bitcoin, Blockchain and Cloud to name a few, and with traditional business models being disrupted (think MP3 players, Camcorders disrupted by Smartphones) and new business models (think Uber/Airbnb, Hyperloop).

However, the COVID – 19 pandemic and the consequent lockdown, restrictions and social distancing, have created far-reaching disruptions of the global economy than ever envisaged. The virtual economy has suddenly altered the projections of the real economy and unsettled nations. The impact of COVID – 19 on our world will be seen in this study, as we progress. Meanwhile, let's look at the lives of leaders.

Many leaders have one standard for their public image and another for their private life

It is easy for leaders, at least in public, to appear as role models. You can fool some people most of the time. However, the people you can't fool, at least for very long, are those in your family. They will see things about you; no one else on the outside will see. How vital that no matter what we profess, our lives must not be lived in contradiction to our profession. This doesn't mean we are perfect; it means only that our family sees the sincerity of our leadership walk, which reveals our real character.

If the motives are pure, life will be pure. The human heart is complicated to understand. Others can judge only on appearance, which, because of the natural duplicity of the heart, rarely corresponds to the real inner condition. Eventually, the mask falls off, and it leaves many who believed and trusted in them disappointed. Thomas Jefferson said, "*I never did, or countenanced, in public life, a single act inconsistent with the strictest good faith; having never believed there was one code of morality for a public, and another for a private man.*" Ethics impacts everything we do, it impacts our relationships, our ability to execute, and ultimately results. Being ethical is not a business concept, or even a management concept, but it is a lifestyle. The more we understand that integrity and accountability is ownership and choice, the more effective we can be in every area in our lives. Real success comes when you're honest with yourself, and with others.

A commitment to responsible leadership is what our world needs. Too many "so-called" leaders ascend into leadership positions for the allure of power.

Sadly, street protests in Venezuela, Brazil, Russia, Iran, Lebanon and many nations in Africa, point to failure of governance. Many leaders are proving irresponsible, and some are unresponsive to the adverse public reactions to their policies.

Leadership is about people. It's about creating a better world for our current and future generations. We need leaders willing to not only help the business grow, but also the people and our communities. With so many disasters and devastation happening around, we want leaders who will genuinely care, who will put people first, and who will make a positive difference. Leaders must embrace their civic duty — the actions of an individual must benefit society. Ultimately, some things must be done because they are the right things to do.

How we interact will change. KPMG recently conducted its annual survey of 800 global technology industry leaders, from start-ups to Fortune 500. The top emerging technology trend that is expected to disrupt business significantly in the next three years is The Internet of Things (IoT). IoT is a network of internet-connected objects able to collect and exchange data using embedded sensors. I expect the highest driver of the use of IoT in business transformation to be improved business efficiencies and productivity, followed by faster innovation cycles. Businesses throughout the world are leveraging their assets, big data, and analytics for an edge over their competitors.

Society is going digital. What is digital transformation? It is a journey of adopting innovative technology and methods.

A Fujitsu report revealed: "89% of organisations are planning, testing, and implementing various digital transformation projects, and 34% of their digital transformation projects had already delivered positive outcomes."

Positioning is critical to getting the highest leverage of your value (skills and capabilities).

Empower employees to drive this change forward.

A company must build adaptive and resilient teams willing to learn new architectures and develop new skill sets.

It starts and ends with people, trust, shared values, vision, and empowerment. The lack of agility in many organisations doesn't impose a new threshold to digital transformation, as a lack of agile decisions affects all kinds of organisational change projects.

Culture is the hardest to change, and it starts at the top. Culture depends on people and relations. Changing a culture is hard and needs a lot of sincerity and authenticity from leaders and not just artificial changes because you have to.

However, culture must submit to change and modernity. In some societies, rigid adherence to archaic cultural practices and traditional belief systems, arrest development and jeopardize progress. Japan has taught the world how traditions and advanced technology continue to develop side by side.

"Culture is the glue that either keeps us doing things well or keeps us doing things poorly." —Professor Ethan Bernstein, Harvard Business School

By being a continuous learner, you will stay ahead of the competition. Learning from experiences is a superior skill in the digital world.

You must create a culture of innovation where continuous improvement and adaptation to change are constant.

Google spent two years studying 180 teams to come up with five key characteristics of enhanced groups. Project Aristotle gathered several of Google's best and brightest to help the organisation codify the secrets to team effectiveness. Through Google's Re:Work website, a resource that shares Google's research, ideas, and practices on people operations, Julia Rosovsky, Google's People Analytics and HR Strategy Leader, outlined the five key characteristics of enhanced teams.

Dependability -	Team members can count on each other to get things done on time.
Structure and Clarity -	High-performing teams have clear goals and roles within the team. *Meaning* - The work has personal significance to each member.
Impact -	The group believes their work is meaningful and is personally relevant to each one of them.
Psychological Safety -	Team members feel safe to take risks on the team without feeling insecure or embarrassed.

Building Block # 3 is a management system that cascades clear strategies and goals through the organisation, with tight feedback loops. The authors said leading companies to embed performance management into the DNA of an organisation from top to bottom and translate top-line goals and priorities into specific metrics and KPIs for employees at all levels.

A culture that prioritises speed and execution over perfection.

Digital transformation focuses on agile business decision making, strategic planning as a continuous process, and people taking centre stage. It must be customer-centric.

Leadership Skill - Develop yourself

Leaders must take strong personal ownership for the development of their digital skills. Don't wait on your company to recommend this for you. The digital transformation put leaders on the spot to develop personal digital skills. Leaders must be *digitally literate*. Seek to raise your technological understanding. This does not mean that to be a successful CEO, you must become a data scientist. You just need to be digitally literate. This includes data literacy, ML literacy, and math literacy, to name a few. It means that to be a successful executive; you need to be familiar with the methods of data science and research.

As the digital world is more numbers-driven, your ability to identify the relevant metrics and be able to think strategically about how to use data to create value for your business is crucial. The complexity of problems has rapidly increased with the digital transformation, while the time available to solve problems has decreased. Aspire to understand the data you collect and the insights you want to extract. The importance for businesses of evaluating and analysing data streams in today's world cannot be emphasised enough. We must design algorithms around specific customer needs.

I recently read an article on *Medium* by Ryan Holmes: "*90% of CEOs Lack This Basic Leadership Skill.*" What skill is it? Social Media. He pointed out that only one in three Fortune 500 CEOs is on *LinkedIn*, to begin with. The rest don't even have a profile.

61% of Fortune 500 CEOs have no social media presence. They're not posting on *LinkedIn*, *Facebook*, *Twitter*, or other networks. He says, *"Considering that social networks are now closing in on 3 billion users – nearly half the global population! – there's something very wrong with that picture."*

The 2016 US presidential election ushered in a new era as much of it was played out in social media. Leaders need to understand the importance of their responsibility as opinion leaders and role models. Leaders should always model *Respect, Civility, Integrity* and *Emotional intelligence* on whatever platform they are on.

Leaders must learn to unlearn old things and discover new ones to stay current and relevant. If you are amid a team who continually says, "That's the way it has always been done here," or "Our business model is bullet-proofed", this is a recipe for disaster. Refusal to catch up with the pace change has been the albatross of yesterday's industrial success stories like Polaroid. Everyone must anticipate change and wake-up up to it. Today's tech giants like Facebook, Apple, Amazon, Microsoft, etc, have created technologies that have changed the way we live and work.

Always focus on the customer experience and look at what digital means through their eyes. It's the best and fastest way to figure things out. Forward-looking leaders understand the seismic shifts that are taking place and quickly adapt. It's about anticipating future trends and customer needs by being aware, predictive, and flexible to the changing marketplace. Visionary innovation beyond customer expectation is critical for survival. It is not enough to ask customers what they need today. You need to spend more time on your thinking to figure out what they need tomorrow. "If I had asked people what they wanted, they would have said faster horses." — Henry Ford.

Here are ten incredible products and services that didn't exist 20 years ago

1   *Android*– Google founder Sergey Brin and engineering director Steve Horowitz debuted Google's Android operating system in November 2007. Today, about 2 billion active devices are running Android software.

2   *Google Chrome*– Google unveiled its Chrome browser on September 1, 2008. "On the surface, we designed a browser window that is streamlined and simple," Google CEO Sundar Pichai wrote on the company's blog.

3   *The iPad*– The iPad was announced as an idea on January 27, 2010, by Steve Jobs at an Apple press conference. The first Apple iPad was thus released on April 3, 2010. Said Jobs: "It's unbelievably great. Way better than a laptop, way better than a smartphone."

4   *Instagram*– First launched in October 2010 with 25,000 people signing up on the first day. By April 2012, Facebook bought the company for $1 billion. Instagram now has approximately 200 million daily active users.

5   *Pinterest*– Pinterest is a visual bookmarking tool and a virtual pinboard. It was founded in March 2010. Today, with 175 million monthly active users, the company is valued at $12 billion.

6   *4G*– 4G networks were an upgrade of the 3G wireless network. First commercially deployed in the Scandinavian countries in 2009, they have only been around for about 11 years. Sprint's HTC Evo was the first 4G phone when it came out in March 2010.

7   *Uber*– Uber is a location-based app that makes hiring an on-demand private driver easy. The company was founded in March 2009. Today, Uber remains the world's most valuable

start-up at about $70 billion, and its business is still growing.

8   *WhatsApp–* WhatsApp was incorporated in 2009 by Brian Acton and Jan Koum, both former employees of Yahoo. WhatsApp is a messaging app. Facebook bought it for $19 billion in 2014.

9   *Kickstarter–* Kickstarter is a platform for launching and backing independent companies and products. Since its inception, 13 million people have supported projects and $3.2 billion has been raised on the site.

10   *Spotify–* Launched in October 2008, in Sweden. They launched a public beta in 2007, but it wasn't until the company signed licensing deals with Universal, Sony, and more that Spotify officially launched. Thirteen years later, Spotify has 140 million active users worldwide.

Just look at today's technology, unimaginable 30 years ago. So, there will be many products and services within the next ten years, ones that we can't begin to imagine, which will revolutionise our world.

If you wait and respond to the changing technology, it won't be long before you're too late.

In the next ten years, there's no guarantee that new products won't emerge from COVID – 19 disruptions to displace today's market leaders.

Companies need to build an innovative culture or die

Amazon, over the years, has increased their releases of new updates or functions, and in 2016, they released over 1,000 new features or innovations. That is over three new functions per day.

Bezos has implemented the culture of innovation.

Is your job or business as safe as you thought it was 30 minutes ago? Being able to anticipate the future instead of reacting to what's happening now will be crucial to survival. Your business and your job are on the line because change is happening so fast.

Just look at the story behind Apple's iTunes. Spotify disrupted iTunes. Yet it was iTunes itself that disrupted the music market. But one upstart disrupted another.

In 1996, Kodak was a titan of an imaging company with a $28 billion market capitalisation and over 140,000 employees. In 2012, they were broke. They still had 17,000 employees, but in the same year that Kodak filed for Chapter 11 bankruptcy protection, Facebook bought Instagram for $1 billion, and they only had 13 employees. Companies with old technologies and ways of thinking will soon be obsolete. Disruption is ruthless and spares no one. The next generation of technology is already here. It is going fast, quick. Even Moore's Law (the expectation for the speed and capability of computers to increase every couple of years, but with consumers paying even less for them with this development) itself is already outdated. We now have Rose's law. Rose's Law for Quantum Computing is a doubling of Moore's law, so it's quadrupling every 12 to 18 months.

Agility and continuous learning are key to success. There is a noticeable gap between the businesses which are thriving and those which are struggling to survive. Far too many of the companies are underestimating the scale of the internal change needed to get this right. Many companies struggle because of the lack of agility and the ability to make the right decisions. Lack of preparedness will probably continue to be the critical issue they face. In the past, digital transformation has been perceived as IT-led and something to compartmentalise in that department. Yet, it will touch all aspects of the business. Companies need to rethink their operating models completely, to adapt and prepare to disrupt or be disrupted.

Embracing agile principles means new ways to work, which require new ways to lead and manage. As with all technology disruptors, it is most important to cultivate and generate a mindset of learning and development in the organisation. Learning organisations quickly get new knowledge and adapt to it. They encourage critical-thinking, disruptive thinking, risk-taking, exploration of new ideas, and welcome feedback to foster innovation. Learning organisations learn from mistakes. They address the knowledge gap and train and coach employees.

Agile as a way of working is changing goals, breaking work down into small slices, changing organisation structures, removing the functional barriers, collaborating more, visualising work, often reflecting, organising the workforce into multidisciplinary teams, and developing cultures of continuous improvement that leverage agile practices. A set of rules guides Amazon's notoriously competitive workplace; one of them is *disagree-and-commit*. Disagree-and-commit is a management principle which states that individuals can disagree -while a decision is being made, but that once a decision has been made, everybody must commit to it. Amazon added, "Have a Backbone; Disagree and Commit" as its 13th leadership principle.

Agility is about building partnerships. Amazon, Apple, Facebook, and Microsoft compete intensely publicly, but behind the scenes, they are cooperating. Everyone uses each other's cloud; Microsoft's software is sought after on the Mac and Windows products are on the Google Play Store.

Microsoft recently announced a deal with Amazon to connect Cortana and Alexa, their voice-activated AI assistants. This news also illustrated how these companies are leveraging their respective strengths.

As Mark Zuckerberg declares on every wall in the Facebook office — "Break things, and move on," and "Done is better than perfect," which inspired people to innovate quickly and to not ask for permission, therefore removing barriers for fast innovation and ideas.

There is no reason not to get started with pilots and prototypes, to learn quickly and adjust as you go. Someone has said that if you want to start something, start anyhow. Do not wait for the perfect time. It may never come. In fact, perfection may be so hard to achieve, that it leads inadvertently to procrastination, which is an unintentional consequence.

An example is *Gmail* — 5 years in iterative beta; Google got the best product-customer fit. See opportunities where others may not. What's impossible today might well be the new healthy tomorrow. The surprises and disruptions around every corner become reminders that the best way forward is to stay in motion.

Our world, as we know it, is changing fast to more of a self-service, on-demand paradigm. Consumerisation of technologies is turning uncertain into certain with the help of modern innovation methods. In our fast-paced world, the risks we must evolve quickly. We just need to make sure we manage those risks so we minimise threats and be able to maximise their potential.

The speed of change is real and is also highlighted by facts like average lifespan of a company in S&P 500 Index (the market index measuring the stock performance of 500 large companies listed on stock exchanges in the US).

According to a new study of turnover in the S&P, conducted by the growth strategy consulting firm *Innosight*, the lifespans of big companies are getting shorter than ever. In 1965, the average tenure of companies on the S&P 500 was 33 years. By 1990, this reduced to 20 years and is forecast to shrink to 14 years by 2026. About half of the S&P 500 companies are expected to be replaced over the next ten years. It is a great strategy to fail small and fast. Working with multiple worldviews or hypotheses simultaneously while developing strategy makes survival possible.

In the famous words of Publilius Syrus (Roman writer, 85BC-43BC), *"Anyone can hold the helm when the sea is calm."* Leading or leadership appears to be a natural, and a given when there are little or no challenges to surmount. This is especially so when things are relatively calm, and all seemed to be at ease. However, when the waves of circumstances creep in stealthily, or rush in with unfathomed temerity, great leadership rises to the challenge, using skills, expertise and ingenious acumen to 'navigate the ship' successfully through the engulfing turbulence.

It convinces many people that new technology will eradicate all our troubles—which is a mere manifestation of wishful thinking.

According to T. S. Eliot and Reinhold Niebuhr—human beings cannot bear much reality, hence the need for "necessary illusions."

Well, before Eliot and Niebuhr, the German philosopher Hans Vaihinger (1852–1933) had already written about these illusions. He developed the philosophy of "as if," —which was published in German as a book in 1911 and translated into English in 1924. In this work, Vaihinger proposes that we should live (as we already do) in a make-believe world. He argued that since reality cannot be indeed known, human beings construct systems of thought to satisfy their needs and then assume that actuality agrees with their constructions; i.e., people act "as if" the real were what they assume it to be.

This indifference is like the initial reaction of one who is diagnosed as having an incurable disease, and then goes through the five stages described by Elizabeth Kubler-Ross in her book On Death and Dying: 1) denial (unconscious or unconscious refusal to accept facts, information, reality); 2) anger (people dealing with emotional upset can be angry with themselves, and/or with others); 3) bargaining (attempting to bargain with God and promises of good behaviour); 4) depression (discouragement); 5) acceptance (peace and realism).

The three laws of motion were compiled by Isaac Newton in his *Philosophiæ Naturalis Principia Mathematica* (Mathematical Principles of Natural Philosophy), first published in 1687. Newton's laws of motion are three physical laws that, together, laid the foundation for classical mechanics. The rules and principles created the foundation for general theories and predictions that could be tested through experiments.

What about social unrest? What about mental issues since most of us connect our self-worth to our jobs? Sigmund Freud, Immanuel Kant and other existentialist philosophers open the door of this behavioural science. Their pioneering work has helped unravel the way the human mind reactions to environmental stimuli.

For Spinoza, Goethe, Hegel, and for Marx, man is alive only since he is productive, because he grasps the world outside of himself expressing his specific human powers, and of understanding the world with these powers. The work of Rene Descartes is worth studying.

In his book, ***The Meaning of Human Existence***, American biologist Edward O. Wilson states that we have four fundamental traits: 1) our instincts are powerful and often brutal; 2) our intelligence is moderate; 3) our wisdom is dangerously limited, and 4) our science is overly confident.

According to Wilson, "*All things being equal (fortunately, things are seldom equal, not exactly), people prefer to be with others who look like them, speak the same dialect and hold the same beliefs. An amplification of this evidently inborn predisposition leads with frightening ease to racism and religious bigotry. Then, also with frightening ease, good people do bad things."*

Here is an analogy of some important events happening around the world. I cannot recall all of them, but I will focus on some of the most important ones drawing on regional dynamics.

(1) France has the most generous tax incentives for R&D in the world. The government is continually expanding the tax credit, and the amount of funding available nearly doubled between 2010 and 2016. A company can receive up to 50 percent of its R&D costs the first year; it covers 40 percent in the second and 30 percent in the third. There is a mechanism that allows funding to be "fast-tracked" for small- and medium-sized enterprises, and in most cases, the waiting period for approval is only three months. Last, the tax credit is either deducted from the annual corporate tax or reimbursed after three years, providing greater flexibility. The tax subsidy rate per $1 of R&D in France averages 43 cents. France recently launched an even more generous package targeting research work in Life Sciences, AI and automotive industries.

(2) Singapore started a Human Capital Development strategy in the 60s. In 1960 Singapore had a per capita GDP of $2,300, roughly equal to Jamaica's. Singapore focused on becoming financial services and research hub, while Jamaica concentrated on tourism. Fifty years later, Singapore's per capita GDP was $43,100, while Jamaica's is slightly above $5,000. Recently, Singapore increased its education subsidy for Life-Sciences and AI and hoping to double the number of scientists in these two critical areas over the next ten years. Singapore has the highest number of scientists on a per capita basis in the world. Today, Singapore is a leader in a host of knowledge-based industries, including the biomedical sciences.

(3) In October 2017, Saudi Arabia unveiled a plan to build a new $500 billion 'Industrial Zone' linked with Jordan and Egypt. Saudi Arabia aims to free the kingdom of dependence on oil exports. The government and private investors will mostly finance it. It appointed former Siemens CEO to lead the project.

(4) China's economy has transformed from a rural agriculture economy to the world's powerhouse in manufacturing in just under 35 years. Today, it is the world's largest producer of ships, high-speed trains, robots, tunnels, computers, bridges, highways, cell-phones, etc. As Napoleon once said, "Let China sleep, for when the dragon awakes, she will shake the world".

It is said that China changes every 24 hours. No wonder, the country is now the No. 2 industrial nation behind the United States.

Both China and India are at the verge of lighting every town and village in the world with their investment in Wind and Solar technologies. In less than five years from today, they will take the world to unlimited energy supply at almost zero cost or a very tiny fraction of what we pay today for electricity consumption and everywhere from Africa to South America will beam with electricity. This is in part responsible for the impending 4th Industrial Revolution that's about to take-off.

Here is the deal driving these jostles and movements around the world causing a country like South Korea (the world's best adopter of technology) to rejig its strategy by renaming its Ministry of Science, ICT and Future Planning to the Ministry of Science, ICT, Future Planning & Innovation. According to the plan, as reported by The Korea Herald, "*the new Science, Technology and Innovation Office will have three bureaus in charge of policymaking for Science and Technology, deliberating R&D investments and testing achievements. The new vice minister-level official to be in charge will be opened for applications from experts in the private sector".*

The world is about to change forever. In the next five to 10 years, all the sectors from manufacturing to retail, to logistics, to the automotive industry to everything is about to be disrupted majorly and shaken to its foundation. We will have unlimited energy, unlimited clean water supply and 80 percent of professional services jobs from Medical to Law, to Aviation, to Transportation, to Logistics, etc. will be replaced by AIs and robots and standard of living and human comfort will shoot up the roof.

The reforms following the impact of the COVID – 19 pandemic will spurn new technologies and cause more disruptions in the virtual space. Industry leaders and government planners should take note of this inevitable change.

My biggest worry is that the government and people of the developing nations (e.g., Nigeria) are hardly aware of what is there. Is merely any strategy in place to take advantage of the innovations knocking at our doors? And we are again in the wrong lane of history. I will give you an example:

While wind, solar and other renewable energy are about to be commercially available, Nigeria, through its Edo Azura project and other similar projects are building 450MW open cycle gas turbine power station with billions of US dollars. The price of Solar has crashed 90 percent over the last two years and will further crash another 90 percent in two or three years and is easier, more portable and safer to deploy. In ten light-years, the world will have no more need for Gas or Crude Oil and the technology to deliver them will become scarce or non-existent.

Summary – Chapter 2

1   The VUCA world is here and has always been here.

2   Planners must respond to the COVID – 19 disruption.

3   The COVID – 19 pandemic may be the foundation of the fifth
    industrial revolution.

4   You can learn from the failure of former successful industries
    that are now extinct.

PART 2

Premium Leadership: The Seven Attributes to Lead and Thrive in a Digitally Transformed VUCA World

"In a world where business leadership has not yet changed its mind-set to the new realities, failures are bound to happen. In this gloomy and hostile situation, leaders should not only just survive but also thrive. This requires shedding old assumptions and gaining new mind sets, being more agile and developing the ability to bounce back from adversity quickly. Behavioural changes, rather than just gaining new competencies and skills, is what I emphasise in this book. Mind you, VUCA is not necessarily doom and gloom. While VUCA can provide threats, it can also offer opportunities, mainly if you translate VUCA as 'vision, understanding, clarity and agility." **(Abidi and Joshi, 2015)**

According to The Latest Research Leadership, Harvard Business Review, April 2020, "Companies of all sorts realise that to survive in today's volatile, uncertain, complex and ambiguous environment, they need leadership skills and organisational capabilities different from those helped them succeed in the past."

The 7 powerful premium new qualities to lead and thrive in the 4th Industrial Revolution VUCA World derived from my over 10 years of practical engagement with both individuals and corporate bodies. This has been underpinned by extensive research across the broader range of research literature and seminal papers. I will now proceed to the crucial part of outlining these new qualities chapter by chapter. To supplement understanding and instil participation, self-practice exercises have been inserted where deemed necessary to facilitate functional understanding and engagement.

Chapter 3

Awareness (Attribute 1)

"Know thyself,"
– Ancient Greek aphorism quoted by Socrates. A moral
injunction to understand your strengths and weaknesses.

There is a Chinese saying: "One disease, long life; no disease, short life." Those who know what's wrong with them and take care of themselves accordingly live a lot longer than those who consider themselves perfectly happy and neglect their weakness.

Absence of profound and broad awareness in leadership lend itself to narrow-mindedness, arrogance, conceit and insecurity, traits that are likely to result in a command-and-control orientation.

In an article titled 'Effective Leadership is an Emotional Experience,' written by Katie Belding and published in THE NORWEST CEO JOURNEY SERIES, she said, "*Know thyself. It's an ancient adage, the basis for bestselling self-help books and therapeutic techniques. Today we have come to accept that self-awareness, empathy, and other attributes that make up emotional intelligence are good things. They contribute to more successful* relationships."

To lead and thrive in today's world, awareness of self, others and the environment that one operates in are very important.

What is Self-Awareness?

According to Allan Twain in his book, 'Self-Awareness: How To Spot And Change Your Behaviour and Disempowering Beliefs with a Proven Step-By-Step Formula for Dramatically Improving Your Self ... Of Your Life' (Twain: The Emotional Series), "*Self-Awareness is all about introspection. This means that you can see yourself as an individual different from other individuals. This also means that you see yourself as a being who lives in this world and that you have certain qualities and characteristics that make you different from others.*

Introspection is also a way of questioning yourself. It means that you can ask yourself about the things you want, what makes you who you are, the things you dislike, your dreams, goals, ambitions and your mistakes, failures and regrets. It is a way of self-psychology.

It could be a way of checking your mental health, and a way of examining your soul."

It is said that the father of modern psychology, William Wundt, was the one who started the whole process of Introspection. Here are the steps of Introspection of Self-Awareness:

Introspection. This is to look within yourself and know how to observe your emotions, thoughts, behaviour and activities throughout the day. You go not only over the positive details but also learn about the negative information.

Detection. Check the patterns in your behaviour that may have caused you sadness, pain, sorrow or regret. You get to hurt yourself and make yourself wallow in sadness even more because of certain habits, but you then realise that you need to chuck off the said habits to become a better person.

Negation. This is about accepting your flaws and harmful patterns for you to take them off your life.

Substitution. This is the act of substituting negative behaviour with positive ones. For examples, envy should be turned into admiration, hate into love, and dishonesty to honesty, etc.

Growing and being happy. When you finally learn how to overcome your bad behaviour, you are a better, more emotionally and mentally stable person who will then grow in happiness and peace. Introspection may seem complicated at first, but in reality, it is one of the simplest ways to help yourself become self-aware and know how to change the bad things that about you. Each one of us has bad habits and behaviour that we need to take out of our lives. In the next chapter, you will learn about the questions that you can ask yourself to know who you are.

"Days of a steam roller type of leader who could aggressively direct the destiny of the organisation are gone, as noted by Jack Welch himself, one of the last such leaders. As a leader, knowing your gaps in self-awareness is one of the essential qualities to possess but also one of the most difficult to gain. The reason is, in most cases, leaders, like everyone else, view themselves in a more favourable light than other people do." **(Abidi and Joshi, 2015)**

A good and effective leader must practice what he preaches. That is why the injunction, "Why do you see the speck in your neighbour's eye, but cannot notice the log in your eye?", lends itself to so much succinct validity.

You are self-aware when you are conscious of and understand your own values, perspectives, strengths, weaknesses, leadership propensities, and emotional needs. (Graham, 2019)

A significant step in becoming an effective leader is to take a good look in the mirror and confidently proclaim that you are a leader yourself. In mastering this awareness or self-leadership, as some people called it, you automatically lay the foundation for assisting others to do the same.

Let us take a quick quiz before proceeding any further.

Which of these should you do first in your quest to lead others?

+ *Bend the will of others to yours by taking a more commanding stance*

+ *Polish your charisma so you can inspire others to do what you want*

+ *Develop an uncanny ability to identify peoples' wants and then incentivise them with these wants to get compliance with whatever it is you demand from them*

+ *Consistently unearth the shortcomings and inadequacies of others*

+ *Castigate them for their failures until they are intimidated to do your bidding*

You are right. None of these entirely meets the pass mark. These may confer a pervasive influence on you, even if only in the short term, but cannot provide a proper foundation for effective leadership.

The first step is to seek genuine awareness by taking a critical look in the mirror to pick out the log in your eye. But you should not limit this awareness to yourself. You must also become acutely aware of others.

A lack of broad and deep awareness makes a leader narrow-minded, arrogant, inward-looking and insecure, and this is likely to result in a command-and-control orientation.

Usually, when we think about leadership, what comes to mind is a leader influencing a follower. When we find ourselves in a position of leadership, our pre-eminent prompting is to think our job is to tell others what to do. In a nutshell, as leaders, we are expected to evaluate the performance of our followers, and to prescribe how they need to improve on that performance, and, naturally, our followers are expected to make themselves amenable to instruction. However, the subject of leadership can be approached from a refreshingly different angle.

The first challenge is to subject ourselves to a session of brutal self-analysis and make necessary readjustments in our world view before even attempting to lead others. For most people, this can be an exceedingly tricky pill to swallow, making this incipient step one subject to the temptation of skipping. Nothing can be more gratifying than identifying problems in other people and proffering solutions to them. Even more attractive is the prospect of commanding and directing others, as this not only massages our ego but makes us feel superior, distinctive and competent.

The very suggestion that, since we believe we are aware of the problems of others, and that we have the solutions to these problems, and can direct those solutions to our problems, can be disconcerting. This is because it is a log that can easily blind us to our shortcomings. We are more inclined to focus on the shortcomings of others, which are almost invariably minor problems, or specks rather than on our big log!

But we ignore our log by presuming that we are the heroes that should direct and control others when we have not yet set aside time to examine our humaneness and shortcomings critically. This translates to bring blinded by a gratifying feeling of power over other people, conveniently enabling us to forget just how flawed we are ourselves.

It predicates the authentic and real foundation of effective leadership upon incisive self-examination, and a genuine willingness to crave self-improvement. A reluctance to engage in this candid and honest self-evaluation and the ameliorative process can see us doing more harm than good in this world.

If we inadvertently create the impression that it is inherently abhorrent to influence and lead others, that would not be entirely accurate. The provision of honest, constructive and ethical leadership is a great act of service. It is just that leadership must be seen as coming from a sincere appreciation of our humaneness. This is a reliable and caring base of humility, and a pragmatic comprehension of that unique human struggle that we all encounter as we make our valiant attempt to be right with our lives and with the world. This presupposes a model of leadership that acknowledges the value of each person and is exercised from an angle of a compassionate sense of caring and an abiding commitment to the well-being of the led. This model of leadership also recognises that each of us is a self-leader.

The personal struggle to learn to lead and motivate constructively, may be at the heart of the search for a life filled with the joy of fulfilment and satisfaction. On a personal note, I have often discovered, much to my delight and humility, that things proceed more satisfactorily the less I try to control, direct and lead. I am humbled to realise that, often, my best work seems to result from those times when I have patiently and sincerely listened, helping people to unravel what is best for themselves, which also means they work out their unique solutions to their problems. I have discovered, in the enlightening process, that when I try to be the all-wise counsellor, expertly forcing my concepts, ideas and knowledge down the throats of others, I am merely intrusive on their journey to authentic self-discovery.

The best teachers, in my humble and carefully considered opinion, are those who acknowledge just how limited their knowledge is, and are consistently prepared to learn and improve themselves. Even better, they insightfully recognise that the real experts are their students and clients, who must live with their challenges every day. In this context, perhaps the more natural way out of the dilemma is to, as much as possible, neutralise those heavy logs that are blinding us, and help others to remove those specks that are standing in the way of the resolution of their own barely hidden solutions. We will end up being of more excellent utility if we humbly assume that most people probably have a far greater grasp of their problem than we do.

Another profound advantage to being more effective leaders is that, not only do we come into a better understanding and empathy for other people and their problems, but we also unwittingly become role models of sorts. Being a role model in this mould does not translate into desiring others to imitate us blindly. Instead, we should strive to be an example of someone who has sincerely and courageously confronted their inadequacies in personal effectiveness and found their safe turf. As a result, we are now in an excellent position to help others discover their turf of efficiency. The highest compliment we can receive is someone giving us feedback, such as, "thank you so much; you do practice what you preach."

This powerful leadership message boils down to the apparent moral that if we don't take the critical step of stepping back to examine ourselves critically, and first lead ourselves effectively, we can be quite easily blinded by this shortcoming. In the circumstances, there is seemingly a huge log of wood blinding us from a clear view of others and their problems. In a nutshell, we need to remove this big log and become right with ourselves, so we can be an example and a source of authentic leadership for others.

In a today's world, a significant impediment to a thorough

appreciation and a proactive attitude to the turbulent times can easily be a combination of self-serving ego, and an inability to cultivate a genuine awareness of our shortcomings.

You must have a conscious awareness of self, and of others which is often referred to as Emotional Intelligence described by Daniel Goleman, Working with Emotional Intelligence as, "The capacity for recognising our feelings and those of others, for motivating ourselves, for managing emotions well in ourselves and in our relationships."

A 2015 article in Fast Company, *'Why emotionally intelligent people are more successful'* by Harvey Deutschendorf cited several studies that claim lack of emotional intelligence is among the primary causes of failure among executives. Conversely, high emotional competency leads to success for people at all levels of an organisation. It has been shown to lead to higher salaries, higher productivity, and higher sales results and even to fewer errors in factory assembly lines.

(Source: *https://www.fastcompany.com/3047455/why-emotionally-intelligent-people-are-more-successful*)

There are many tools out there for you to develop self-awareness if you want to. They include:

- MBTi
- Johari Window
- 360 feedback
- Informal feedback
- Analysis of performance
- Skills analysis
- Personalist Test. You can take a FREE TEST @ https://www.16personalities.com/. It takes less than 12 minutes.

In his acclaimed study *"The Iceberg of Ignorance"*, consultant Sidney Yoshida concluded: *"Only 4% of an organisation's frontline problems are known by top management, 9% are known by middle management, 74% by supervisors and 100% by employees..."*

You must also develop an awareness of your immediate environment using tools like SWOT Analysis and PESTLE Analysis.

According to Lao Tzu, "Mastering others is strength. Mastering yourself is true power."

How to Develop Self-Awareness

Develop a daily self-reflection practice. Make time for adequate introspection. Don't make sudden decisions. Pause and listen to yourself and pause and listen to others. Name and understand personal emotions rather than transferring them to others. Recognise and consider what is at the root of a feeling or emotion before reacting to an employee or making a hasty decision. Maintain a journal of emotions to recognise your feelings' patterns over time and use the insights to mould your reactions effectively. Ask peers for feedback. Get feedback about your leadership style from those you work with, listen to what people say, and implement these changes into your life. Do you engage with your direct reports to get 360-degree professional feedback? Do you set monthly, quarterly, or annual goals for improvement and personal development?

This can help reveal some blind spots that you may have. Be open to uncomfortable feelings or feedback without reacting in adverse ways. Filter your thoughts before you put them to action.

<u>Source</u>: *The Future of Leadership: Rise of Automation, Robotics and Artificial Intelligence by Brigette Tasha Hyacinth (2018)*

Authenticity

One thing that having a deep self-awareness will enable you to be is the real you. Be authentic.

Authenticity is being genuine, real, and veritable, in sharing the sense of actuality and lack of falsehood or misrepresentation.

In recent times, upheavals in society have energised a tremendous demand for authentic leadership. The destruction on 9/11, corporate scandals at companies like WorldCom, Enron, Tesco and massive failures in the banking industry have all created fear and uncertainty.

People feel apprehensive and insecure about what is going on around them, and, as a result, they long for bona fide leadership they can trust and for leaders who are honest and competent.

A vision is what an organisation wishes to be like in some years' time. A mental picture of the future. It is a constant force and a critical anchor that drives decisions, actions and judgments.

"The very essence of leadership is that you have to have a vision." - Father Theodore Hesburgh

One of my favourite stories is when John F. Kennedy visited the NASA Space Centre, he saw a janitor carrying a broom, and he walked over and asked what he was doing. The janitor responded, "Mr President, I'm helping put a man on the moon."

Although Kennedy was already dead when the Apollo II landed on the moon in 1969, his vision has inspired other nations to join the quest for space exploration; originally triggered by the defunct Soviet Union, which pioneered space exploration when they put the first man, Yuri Gargarin, in orbit.

To be authentic, you must have a *Vision.*

Vision is a constant force. It is a critical anchor that drives decisions, actions and judgments. With a younger workforce that is purpose-driven, having a compelling vision for the future is also a key driver of engaging and keeping high-performing team members. A compelling vision is an essential pre-requisite for any community or network to succeed. Leaders who will thrive in a VUCA future are the ones who have a clear vision of where they want their organisations and teams to be.

ENFORCERS OF CHANGE

Matthew Ashimolowo, the Nigerian clergyman and senior pastor of Kingsway International Christian Centre (KICC) in London illustrates change enforcement succinctly in his book, '*35 Marks of Irrepressible Leadership: Unique qualities for unsurpassable, powerful and passionate leadership. Habits of leaders who change their world.*'

"Dubai, in the United Arab Emirates, used to be a desert covered with dunes. Its seaport, having been in operation from the days of the Arabian tales, was limited in its scope, capacity and output. Kings came and left. Kingdoms conquered and changed the horizon several times. The British too were involved. However, the most significant change to Dubai was with Sheik Maktoum who saw the possibilities of this desert island becoming the playground of the world, the greatest trade zone of the Middle East, a place where architectural feats would meet with a global display of wealth. The rest is history. Not only did Sheik Maktoum see this vision, but he also enforced it and challenged those who followed him to see the same and make it happen."

(Source: Ashimolowo, M. *35 Marks of Irrepressible Leadership: Unique qualities for unsurpassable, powerful and passionate leadership. Habits of leaders who change their world* (2015). Riverblue Publishing. London (UK), 121 pages)

Another man who had a vision and was able to enforce it, is the Ayatollah Ruhollah Khomeini of Iran. His Islamic revolution swept off the Shah Rava Parllahvi ruling dynasty of Iran, because his followers enforced his beliefs.

Here's another brilliant reference. In his bestselling book '*True North: Discover Your Authentic Leadership*', Bill George, Former Chairman and Chief Executive Officer, Medtronic, Inc. and Professor of Management Practice, Harvard Business School affirmed, "*The reality is that no one can be authentic by trying to be like someone else. You can learn from the experiences of others, but there is no way you can be successful in trying to be like them. People trust you when you are genuine and authentic, not an imitation.*"

Based on his experience as a corporate executive and through interviews with a diverse sample of 125 successful leaders, George found that authentic leaders have a genuine desire to serve others, they know themselves, and they lead from their core values. Specifically, authentic leaders demonstrate five essential characteristics:

(1) They understand their purpose,

(2) they have strong values about the right thing to do,

(3) they establish trusting relationships with others,

(4) they demonstrate self-discipline and act on their values, and

(5) they are passionate about their mission (i.e., act from their heart)

In his interviews, George found that authentic leaders have a real sense of purpose. They know what they are about and where they are going. Besides knowing their purpose, authentic leaders are inspired and intrinsically motivated about their goals. They are passionate individuals who have a deep-seated interest in what they are doing and genuinely care about their work.

A good example of an authentic leader who exhibited passion about his goals was Terry Fox, a cancer survivor, whose leg was amputated after it was overcome by bone cancer. Using a special leg prosthesis, Terry Fox attempted to run across Canada, from the Atlantic to the Pacific, to raise awareness and money for cancer research. Although Terry died before he finished his run, his courage and passion affected the lives of millions of people. He also accomplished his goals to increase cancer awareness and to raise money for cancer research.

Today, the **Terry Fox Foundation** is going strong and has raised more than $400 million

(Canadian) for cancer research (***http://www.terryfoxrun.org***). Of the dimensions and characteristics of an authentic leader, Terry Fox showed purpose and passion in his leadership.

Authentic leaders understand their values and behave toward others based on these values. Stated another way, George suggests that authentic leaders know their **"True North."**

They have a clear idea of who they are, where they are going, and what the right thing is to do. When tested under challenging situations, authentic leaders do not compromise their values but use those situations to strengthen their values.

An example of a leader with a robust set of values is Nobel Peace Prize Laureate Nelson Mandela.

Mandela is a profoundly moral man with a healthy conscience. While fighting to abolish apartheid in South Africa, he was unyielding in his pursuit of justice and equality for all. When he was in prison and offered an early release for denouncing his viewpoint, he remained incarcerated rather than compromise his position. Nelson Mandela knew who he was at his core. He knew his values, and his leadership reflected those values.

Mandela gave the world a template for moral leadership. Coming from Africa, it was refreshing because that continent is known for corrupt, sit-tight and irresponsible leadership.

The third characteristic of authentic leadership in the George approach is strong relationships. Authentic leaders can open themselves up and establish a connection with others. They will share their own story with others and listen to others' stories. Through mutual disclosure, leaders and subordinates develop a sense of trust and closeness. George argued that people today want to have access to their leaders, and they want their leaders to be open with them. People are asking leaders to soften the boundary around their leadership role and to be more transparent. People want to have a trusting relationship with their leaders. In exchange, people will give leaders greater loyalty and commitment.

With a younger workforce that is purpose-driven, being authentic and having a compelling vision for the future is also a key driver of engaging and keeping high-performing team members. A compelling vision is an essential pre-requisite for any community or network to succeed. Leaders who will thrive in today's world are the ones who have a clear vision of where they want their organisations and teams to be.

The book, *'Finding Your True North: A Personal Guide'* by Bill George, Andrew McLean & Nick Craig, gives a breakdown of the five things required to be authentic as a leader.

1. Do you understand your PURPOSE?

2. Do you have and practice solid VALUES

3. Are you leading with HEART?

4. Do you show SELF-DISCIPLINE

5. Are you building and establishing enduring RELATIONSHIPS?

How can you achieve the five things above as a leader?

(1) They understand their purpose,

Let us start with purpose?

- What is your purpose as a leader and do you have a purpose statement for your organisation?
- It starts with WHY?
- Leading with Purpose requires self-awareness, which is the cornerstone of authentic leadership development

Key questions/prompts:

- Why are you doing what you're doing?
- What drives you?
- Do you have a clear sense of direction?

EXERCISE: Give people a couple of minutes to answer this question and make a note in their workbook. List all the reasons, everything from 'to make a difference–salary'. They will do more work on purpose and passion for later exercises.

Examples of companies with a powerful purpose statement:

- "Nourishing families so they can flourish and thrive"– **Kellogg's**
- "To help people manage risk and recover from the hardship of unexpected loss"–**International Airlines Group**
- "To put a smile on the face of everyone we touch"–**Nintendo**
- "To create a better everyday life for the many people"–**IKEA**
- "To bring inspiration and innovation to every athlete in the world"–**Nike**

- "To inspire and nurture the human spirit—one person, one cup and one neighbour at a time"–**Starbucks**

- "To refresh the world in mind, body and spirit. To inspire moments of optimism and happiness through our brands and actions. To create value and make a difference"–**Coca-Cola.**

- "To embrace the human spirit and let it fly"–**Virgin Atlantic**

(Source: O'Brien, J. and Cave, A., 2017. *The Power of Purpose: Inspire teams, engage customers, transform business.* **Pearson UK.)**

(2) They have strong values about the right thing to do,

Values are our moral compass and the deeply held beliefs that guide your actions:

- What is important to you about your work?

- How do you behave under pressure?

Leading through Values comes through developing clarity about your values, leadership principles, and ethical boundaries.

Life Purpose Inventory: Identify your core values

- Identify your work and career values

- Rank them in order of greatest importance

EXERCISE: Work in pairs. At each pause, **they** ask, 'What else is important to you in your work and career? What else? What else?' B–Says out loud all those things important to them in their work and career. Watch out for people listing things that they THINK should be on their list but that they never demonstrate in real life.

Additional questions:

- Where are you experiencing value conflicts?
- What can you do to resolve the conflicts?
- When do you knowingly ignore your values?
- Translate your values into leadership principles (I will _____)

"The softest pillow is a clear conscience." **Narayana Murthy, Founder and CEO of Infosys.**

Achievement	Fulfilment	Knowledge	Security
Adventure	Fun	Leadership	Self-discipline
Beauty	Fitness	Learning	Self-esteem
Charity	Freedom	Love	Service
Community	Generosity	Loyalty	Spirituality
Compassion	Happiness	Nature	Status
Creativity	Health	Passion	Strength
Dignity	Honesty	Patriotism	Supportiveness
Discipline	Honour	Peace	Sensitivity
Excellence	Humility	Power	Time
Experience	Independence	Perfection	Truth
Faith	Individuality	Pride	Trust
Family	Integrity	Reason	Winning
Finance	Justice	Respect	Wisdom
Friendship	Kindness	Recognition	Working

- Prioritise your values
- Write a list of 7 words that are some things or values that are most important to you in life, business or career
- Add words important to you to the list
- From the list pick seven values that represent you and your business
- Spend a few minutes interpreting your values and what they mean to you and your business
- Prioritise your values and place them in order of importance
- Is it consistent with your VALUES?

(3) They establish trusting relationships with others,

- How can you develop long-lasting and enduring relationships in many relationships?

(4) They show self-discipline and act on their values, and

- Do you set high standards?
- Do you hold yourself and others accountable for their performance?
- Do you admit mistakes and start corrective action?

(5) They are passionate about their mission (i.e., act from their heart)

- Do you have a passion for your work?
- Do you have compassion for the people you serve?
- Do you have empathy for those you work with?

LIFE PURPOSE INVENTORY

Go through the list of words and phrases below and circle all the items that give you a strong positive feeling. Remember, there are no correct answers, and the meaning of each word and phrase is for you to determine.

Personal Achievement	Winning
Happiness	Finding the good in others
Earning money	Gaining recognition
Loving someone (others)	Building something
Being loved, being accepted	Gaining the approval of others
Popularity	Creating something
Competence	Getting things done
Independence	Doing good
Risking	Dominating
Being different and still fitting in	Being unique
Being your best	Being the best
Reaching your potential	Gaining security, safety
Finding excitement	Controlling
Being a leader	Having fun
Learning, gaining wisdom	Working hard
Gaining mastery	Having influence over others
Making a worthwhile contribution	Experiencing life to its fullest
Fully expressing yourself	Seeking adventure
Becoming an expert	Power, authority
Making a positive difference	Prestige
Developing people or things	Increasing effectiveness
Seeing what you can get away with	Waiting until the last minute

(If a word or phrase comes to mind that isn't on the list, please add it)

They have strong values, about the right thing to do,

Note: Add information on how to discover and live your values

Identifying your core values

- Identify your work and career values
- Rank them in order of most importance
- Review the top 5 in more detail:
- – What does each value mean to you?
- – Why is it important?

WORK AND CAREER VALUES

Look at the things you have circled on the previous page - What is important to you about your work and career?

For example: Making a difference, achievement, having fun, progressing, new challenges, learning, inspiring others, responsibility, reaching my potential. Write one word or phrase per line.

_____

_____

_____

_____

_____

Go back and rank your top 8 career values, 1= the most important.

Review the top 5 in more detail:

- What does each value/word mean to you?
- Why is it important?

Green Peak Partners and Cornell University examined seventy-two executives at public and private companies with revenues from $50 million to $5 billion. They found that the strongest predictor of overall success was high self-awareness. Those who have high self-awareness have the foundation for: Enhancing their performance, Clarifying their purpose and direction, Overcoming labels (race, gender, circumstance), Growing and learning Developing leadership skills and Honing emotional intelligence (Cooper, 2016)

Summary – Chapter 3

1 Having self-awareness is important

2 Purpose, vision and values are the core determinants of good leadership.

3 Vision can only be successful, if enforced.

4 There is no perfect time to start. Just hit the ground running, perfection will follow.

5 Study the charts and apply what they teach.

Chapter 4

Anticipation (Attribute 2)

One of the qualities needed to lead in a *VUCAlised* 4th Industrial Revolution is *Anticipate,* which is the ability to spot trends and connect the dots. It is having a Strategic Perspective. You must be able to anticipate and see the future. Some people describe it as being able to "see around the corner."

Leadership development and strength building have been the focus of experts and professionals alike. One such example is Jack Zenger, the CEO of Zenger/Folkman, a strength-based leadership development firm. Jack is a serial author and co-author of more than a dozen books. In an article in **Forbes**, '*The 6 Competencies Global Leaders Need To Succeed*', Jack, in writing about leadership development and building strengths stated:

"Colleagues describe them as being able to 'see around the corner.' Looking at the same data that others have available, the best global executives were able to identify issues that others pass by or ignore. For example, one executive in Mexico noticed that monthly revenue had

declined. He had seen variations before, so this was not unexpected. Nevertheless, this seemed different. He called a few friends in other companies and asked if they had seen the same trend. To his surprise, all had observed the trend but thought nothing of it.

After consulting with several economists and other company financial executives, he called and indicated that he was going to delay a planned expansion. While he did not know it at the time, he had predicted a significant economic slowdown. Foresight is when you can predict what's likely to happen in the future by learning from past experiences, identifying what's happening now, and understanding the consequences of your decisions."

He added further: *"Strategic Perspective. These executives have a much clearer view of the future of the company. Their deep industry and culture knowledge enable them to be much better at anticipating market and economic trends. They take a longer-term view of the business and the market, as well as taking the broad strategy and translating it into meaningful goals and objectives in their organisations."*

(Source: https://www.forbes.com/sites/jackzenger/2014/06/26/the-6-competencies-global-leaders-need-to-succeed/#52344fcb56f1 (accessed Wednesday 15 April 2020 2128 hours)

The best time to plan is when things are good, not when crisis set in. If most businesses had strengthened their online platforms, they would not have been so devastated when COVID - 19 struck, forcing many fragile companies which have collapsed to fold-up.

Thinking Differently

Thomas Edison once said, "Thinking is the hardest discipline of all."

In 2002, I met Sir Richard Branson at his then residence at Holland Park in London through Africa's celebrity magazine, *Ovation,* published by Dr. Dele Momodu. After the press conference to announce the then Virgin Atlantic London to Port Harcourt flight, Sir Richard hosted us for drinks in his garden. During the drinks reception, I walked up to him and asked, "Sir Richard, please what is the secret of success apart from hard work, perseverance and determination?" He responded, "Ability to think and do things differently from the others."

Thinking differently and having the courage of conviction is an essential law of success as a leader in a VUCA world and the Fourth Industrial Revolution. As a leader and to thrive in today's world, you must be able to think and do things differently from the others. You must look at causing disruptions in the marketplace.

Apple

When you look at where Apple is now, it is easy to forget where the company was in the mid-1990s. It had lost ground massively to Microsoft and was a minor player in the IT marketplace. No less a figure than Michael Dell back in 1995 had said that he would have closed the company down if he were running it. Steve Jobs thought differently though when he returned in 1997 to take the reins again of the company he founded. In fact, "Think Different" was the title of an advertising campaign that Apple ran soon after he returned.

(Source: *Face It & Fix It: How to Avoid Disaster and Turn Around Your Small Business* by Mac Attram)

Los Angeles ad agency TBWA/Chiat/Day created Apple television and print advertising campaign that turned into one of the most famous campaigns in corporate history. "*Think Different*" debuted on September 28, 1997, and became an instant classic. As black-and-white images of celebrated iconoclasts filled the screen (Albert Einstein, Martin Luther King, Richard Branson, John

Lennon, Amelia Earhart, Muhammed Ali, Lucille Ball, Bob Dylan and others), actor Richard Dreyfuss voiced the narration:

"Here's to the crazy ones. The misfits. The rebels. The trouble makers. The round pegs in the square hole. The ones who see things differently. They're not fond of rules. And they have no respect for the status quo. You can quote them, disagree with them. Because they change things. They push humans forward. And while some may see them as the crazy ones, we see genius. Because the people who are crazy enough to think can change the world and the ones who do."

The campaign won a ton of awards, became a cult favourite and lasted five years, which is an eternity in the life cycle of ad campaigns. The campaign reinvigorated the public's appetite for all things Apple, including an interest in one of the most influential iconoclasts in the computer world, Steve Jobs himself.

That phrase encapsulates what Steve Jobs did to turn around the fortunes of the iconic tech company. How did he do it? He thought differently, he innovated, and he wasn't afraid to be controversial. The turnaround he engineered is nothing short of outstanding. In his time there, the stock price increased by over 8,500% and revenues increased by over 820%.

Here are five ways that Steve jobs went about his job

1   *He hated mundane products.* Jobs made sure that Apple's products were not only innovative in and of themselves, but he also ensured that they were integrated. So, iPods, iPads, iTunes, iPhone and the App Store were all engineered to work together.

2   *He knew that customers don't always know what they want.* Apple doesn't run focus groups. It has a track record of intuitively creating new products and then persuading

customers to buy those products that they wouldn't previously have thought they wanted.

3   *Jobs wasn't afraid to go back to basics and change what the company was all about.* It began as a computer company, but Jobs broadened out Apple's product offerings. To symbolise this transformation, the company's name was changed in 2007 from Apple Computer, Inc. to Apple Inc.

4   *He wasn't afraid to break with convention.* Traditionally tech companies have not been retailers. But Steve Jobs wasn't happy with how stores were positioning and merchandising Apple's products. So, Jobs got into retail and create Apple Store. He did retail differently, and the shops have become hugely successful and have shaken up how retail is done.

5   *Jobs knew the massive importance of aesthetics.* Computer products historically had never looked right. The function had always come before form. Apple changed that by making their products look beautiful. Jobs knew that if he could make them desirable objects, then they would fly off the shelves. It started with iMac being colourful and has continued with the sleekness and desirability of how iPods, iPhone and iPad look and feel. Jobs was never afraid to try anything. Apple and Microsoft were sworn enemies, just like Coca-Cola and Pepsi. But when Jobs took over the company again in 1997, it had been losing money for 12 years. So, what did Steve Jobs do? He approached Bill Gates and what followed was a $150 million investment into Apple. That enabled Apple to achieve financial stability finally. Both companies ended up winners when they previously had been fierce competitors.

(Source: *Face It & Fix It: How to Avoid Disaster and Turn Around Your Small Business* by Mac Attram)

Steve Jobs was the prophetic brain of America tech companies. He was a man who saw and lived in the future. But the greatest lesson he taught the world is never to give up, even when you fall.

How Levi Roots' thinking altered his fortune

I interviewed London-based musician-turned-businessman Levi Roots on my TV programme in 2007. When I asked him his secret of slaying the dragon on the TV programme, ***Dragon's Den***, he said: *"A big part of my armoury and my secret weapon to slay the Dragons, was my guitar and singing my 'sauce song' live on the show. It's never been done before... First Rasta man too."*

"Put some music in my food for me, gimme some Reggae Reggae sauce... Hot Reggae Reggae sauce, It's so nice I had to name it twice... gimme some Reggae Reggae sauce..."

'I like you Levi, and I think the sauce is great too.' Peter went on....Telling me how he wouldn't buy Reggae Reggae Sauce if it weren't for me selling it to him. He commented on my dress sense and presentation before only offering half of my asking price of 50,000 for 20% of my business. He wanted the whole lot; 20% share for £25,000". His company is now worth £8million

He said, *"On the day we filmed Dragons' Den on Tuesday 9th January 2007, I was down to my last £20. I gave £10 to the taxi driver who dropped me off at the studios. I had been working as a salesman in a builders' merchants, selling plumbing equipment, but I gave that up because I wanted to develop my business. I was taking a risk – I didn't know what would happen, but something was telling me to follow my dreams. I started exhibiting my sauce at trade exhibitions, and luckily, I was spotted by the BBC at the World Food Market exhibition in Docklands".*

As at today the world's biggest payments network, Bitcoin has no cash. The world's largest taxi company founded by the duo of Travis Kalanick owns no vehicles. According to https://www.uber.com/en-GB/newsroom/history/, on a snowy Paris evening in 2008, Travis Kalanick and Garrett Camp had trouble hailing a cab. So, they came up with a simple idea – tap a button, get a ride. What started as an app to request premium black cars in a few metropolitan areas is now changing the logistical fabric of cities around the world.

The world's most popular media owner creates no contents. The world's most valuable retailer founded by Mark Zuckerberg, along with fellow Harvard College students and roommates, Eduardo Saverin, Andrew McCollum, Dustin Moskovitz, and Chris Hughes has no inventory. The world's largest accommodation provider founded by the trio of Joe Gebbia, Brian Chesky and Nathan Blecharczyk owns no real estate. One thing all the founders have in common is that they could think and do things differently from other entrepreneurs.

David Bohm, the theoretical physicist, famously stated: "*The ability to perceive and think differently is more important than the knowledge gained.*"

At the core of thinking differently is innovation. Your education, background and upbringing can condition the way you think about and think through a problem. It is about developing an expansive mind and growth mindset.

Innovation is at the core of thinking differently, and I will use the story of **SAMSUNG.**

The Early Years of Samsung

Born out of the larger Samsung chaebol was in the food-processing and textiles sectors, Samsung Electronics started in 1969, manufacturing low-cost black and white TVs, fridges, microwaves, and washing machines. (A South Korean word meaning business association, the chaebol are large, conglomerate family-controlled firms).

Although by the early 1990s Samsung Electronics had grown to be a significant manufacturer with its products sold around the world, at heart this firm was still producing low-end products and, in its part of the market, was facing increasing competition. To grow, it needed to continue to win in its core area but also move upmarket and compete at a higher level.

According to company lore, in 1993 Kun-Hee Lee, chairman of Samsung Electronics, visited an electronics store in Los Angeles and was struck because its products were viewed as a cheap commodity. Although good value at the low end of the market, they were not seen to be in the same class as products from competitors such as Sony that stood out on the shop floor and were given premium positioning. The lack of a coherent design identity was highlighted as a significant weakness for Samsung Electronics, compared to Sony and Philips, where the design was seen as a core corporate asset. Samsung Electronics recognised that, if it was to grow, design quality should play a leading role in its organisation alongside technology leadership. The chairman made things clear: "*Management is still clinging to the concept of quantity at the expense of quality. We will become a third-rate company. We must change, no matter what.*" He got everybody to think differently. He then famously said: "*change everything except your wife and kids.*"

The book, *Growth Champions: The Battle for Sustained Innovation Leadership (Growth Agenda, 2012)* highlights the meteoric rise of electronics giants, Samsung and their almost mythical transition to the digital world.

Samsung Electronics is the world's largest consumer electronics company. Producing everything from phones, TVs, cameras, and laptops to microwaves and freezers, it is a top-three brand in pretty much every category in which it is active. 2010 sales were more than $135 billion, with net profits of over $14 billion. Samsung Electronics is now twice the size of Sony, the company which 20 years ago was the undisputed leader in the sector. While Sony's revenues grew by 22% total in the last decade, Samsung Electronics' revenue rose by over 400% and, over the past five years, the company has maintained growth at an average of 16% every year.

In the TV market, Samsung Electronics has been a market leader by a good margin over Sony and local rival LG since 2006 and is way ahead in LCD panels; in the camera market it is number 2 to Sony and despite intense competition; in the cell phone market, Samsung Electronics has just over 20% of the global market and is rapidly closing in on Nokia.

Today Samsung Group revenue is $200 billion, and it accounts for a fifth of Korea's exports.

Samsung has become the flagship of the South Korean economy and the source of much of the innovation that is taking place across the consumer electronics sector. Given that it was a low-cost 'me-too' manufacturer of imitations of Sharp's microwaves in the 1970s, this is a considerable achievement.

Whereas people used to look at Philips, Sony, and Toshiba for the latest developments, today it is Apple and Samsung Electronics. As Apple has moved across some consumer electronics markets with its high margin products; it has become the only real challenger to Samsung's dominance. Pivotal to Samsung Electronics' success over the past decade has been the way it has embraced design as the source of competition.

Product image and innovation combined to spell success for Samsung. Its ability to learn quickly and adapt to changes, helped to expand its range and appeal. That's why it has become a global brand leader.

(Source: *Growth Champions: The Battle for Sustained Innovation Leadership (Growth Agenda)*. 2012. Edited by Tim Jones (Editor),☐ Dave McCormick (Editor),☐ Caroline Dewing (Editor)

How to Think Differently

In this fast-changing world, we need to balance how to think differently with how to grow expertise. To think differently, we need to be good at thinking. To think differently, you need to be conscious of where your intellectual and emotional energies are invested and when to switch. **But to think differently, you must think well**. Being smart becomes your platform, your expertise. To do that though, we need to change something fundamental to how we function. Can we rebalance between thinking fast and slow?

(Credit: '*How To Think Differently (And Why!)*' by Haydn Shaughnessy)

To think differently, develop what we call the *growth mindset*.

What is Mindset?

What is the mindset? According to world-renowned Stanford psychologist Carol Dweck, it is an established set of attitudes or beliefs. We all know instinctively that attitude is essential, but Dweck argues that it is everything.

After studying the behaviour of thousands of children, Dr. Dweck coined the terms **fixed mindset** and **growth mindset** to describe the underlying beliefs people have about learning and intelligence. When students believe they can get smarter, they understand that effort makes them more durable.

She explains why it's not just our abilities and talent that bring us success—but whether we approach them with a fixed or growth mindset. A fixed mindset is one in which you view your talents and abilities as… well, fixed. You are who you are, your intelligence and talents are what they are, and your fate is to go through life, avoiding challenge and failure.

In a fixed mindset, people believe their basic qualities, like their intelligence or talent, are simply fixed traits. They spend their time documenting their intelligence or ability instead of developing them. They also believe that talent alone creates success—without effort. They're wrong.

In a **growth mindset,** people believe that they can develop their most basic abilities through dedication and hard work— brains and talent are just the starting point. This view creates a love of learning and a resilience essential for great accomplishment. Virtually all great people have had these qualities.

Mindset is the key to progress in any aspect of human endeavour; it is what undergirds successful outcomes. But it depends on which mindset we adopt. As clearly explained by Dr. Dweck, you grow if you grow the mindset; you stagnate if you chose to have a fixed mindset.

Sources: https://www.mindsetonline.com/whatisit/themindsets/index.html

They raise many of us with a fixed mindset, but to develop and think differently, we must embrace and develop a growth mindset.

2.   *Experiment to see differently*

An article in The Garage Group (www.the garagegroup.com) puts this succinctly: *"Michael Dell took computers apart at age 15 to understand how they worked... the process of experimentation and building and rebuilding gave him a vision for Dell and his disruptive direct-to-consumer business model. This could look like learning a new skill, taking something apart and putting it back together. Look for insights into how things work, fit together, support or interrupt each other."*

(Credit: http://www.thegaragegroup.com/6-steps-to-amp-up-your-associative-thinking-skills/)

3.   *Question everything*

A few years ago, Bill Jensen wrote a fantastic book, *'Disrupt: Think Epic. Be Epic: 25 Successful Habits for an Extremely Disruptive World.'* His habit No 1 is 'Question Everything'. He said, *"Ask the questions no one is asking. Many of our systems, structures, rules and approaches are holdovers from the Industrial Age and need to be completely rethought"*.

4.   *Another is to develop associative thinking*

Associative thinking is the mental process of making associations between a subject and all present pertinent factors without drawing on experience. Free association. Thinking in a manner that makes associations is a powerful tool. We are all raised with a specific perspective and specific associative skills. **Dyer, Gregersen & Christensen** in their book *"The Innovator's DNA: Mastering the Five Skills of Disruptive Innovators"* point out that a lot of innovation comes back to associative thinking, or can be, a learned skill. That is to say, it happens when we mash up a lot of ideas or sources of information.

5.   *Go on a low information diet.*

A term popularised by Tim Ferris in his bestselling book 'The 4-Hour Work Week,' it is having minimal access to news and information for a while. Also, avoid information that doesn't 'concern me'. Because information overload is a plague of the 21st century.

6.   *Practice mindfulness*

What is Mindfulness? According to *mindfulness.org*, *"Mindfulness is the basic human ability to be fully present, aware* *of where we are and what we're doing, and not overly reactive or overwhelmed by what's going on around us"*. A mental state achieved by focusing one's awareness on the present moment, while calmly acknowledging and accepting one's feelings, thoughts, and bodily sensations, used as a therapeutic technique.

7. *Develop ability consciousness*

Ability-conscious leaders will need to recognise and prepare for the VUCA world. They will have to handle a fast-paced and speeding up work environment. These leaders need to be competent at finding learning opportunities, evaluate their experiences and then apply that learning to their environments. Intellect will be critical to provide analysis, insightful judgement and to deal effectively with complex and ambiguous information. Finally, these leaders will need to be action-oriented, enthusiastic and driven for results more than ever before.

As one leader pointed out, "the customised news feeds we all enjoy can generate blinkers on the sides of our heads and constrain our views." Therefore, he makes a point of reading outside his typical areas of interest to remove the blinkers and broaden his horizons.

It is an indubitable fact that as we ask the right questions, we will make better decisions. Refusing to do so risks putting leaders outside their "uncomfortable comfort zones," thus exposing them to the danger of decision paralysis.

One of the best things that can happen to a leader is having people around him to tell how wrong he is. If leaders report feeling residual anxiety despite useful information, many turn to peer mentoring or benchmarking for validation. In the words of one leader, seeking validation means "sharing your problem and being vulnerable with people that otherwise you might be uncomfortable doing that with." Validation is critical for tempering doubt and channelling its productive uses.

It is instructive that even those leaders who feel well informed value the friction and the debate that goes on around them, no matter how seemingly insignificant they may be. This disallows them getting too comfortable and overconfident. Such leaders often create environments where honest and constructive debate is not only welcome but expected. Such leaders are well-positioned to leverage the diversity of thought that can lead to better and more thoughtful challenges to the status quo.

It is when constructive conflict is present that an angle, a perspective or a vision that was not previously that clear suddenly becomes clear.

It is also right that some leaders who are comfortable deciding with limited information often rely on experience or gut instinct. However, even they will readily acknowledge that in new situations where their gut may be wrong, it remains imperative to marry that gut feeling with the ability to be humble enough to ask. Leaders in this category rely on traditional risk-management approaches to protect against the negative consequences of their decisions. This helps give them a sense of preparation while safeguarding against the hubris that the "CEO knows best." A leader must be conscientious. Because if you are not careful and you think that you are indestructible, then that's where the dangers lurk.

In honing their abilities to think differently, leaders also need to listen to other voices. "One of the biggest lessons to me," noted a corporate leader, "is the deliberate effort to listen to the organisation; it's easy to pretend to listen."

An important skill is the ability to ask the right questions and of one-to-one communications, being both informational and motivational. The debate can enrich by highlighting the fact that leaders are not infallible.

Leaders must be learners. They continue to learn and grow, progressing through a series of phases that correspond to their response to new challenges. *"There's no way you know everything,"* said one company executive, *"You always have to continue to learn, and there's always somebody that's faced the problem or challenge that you're about to face. You can learn from those folks. We're all lonely at the top together."*

Curiosity is a trait that leaders need to hone until it becomes a discipline. A leader must have an enormous mindset of openness and learning because however much of a genius you think you are, you are still not a genius. You must always believe (that) you've still got a lot to learn, and you can learn from everybody.

There are various methods you can use to sustain curiosity. These include reading widely, talking to a wide range of interest groups, exploring areas that are not necessarily ones you are interested in.

It is also of the most compelling importance to continue to update your core professional knowledge base and to let go of doing things you were good at and enjoyed and doing something that you are no good or competent at, but which your organisation needs you to do.

Ultimately, this is the mindset that can help propel leaders up the various cycles of growth they will encounter along the way in their roles, even as these roles continue to evolve in unexpected ways. Whether it's mastering new capabilities, developing new forms of competitive intelligence, or learning to make ethical choices, the leaders of our new VUCA world will embody this spirit of growth, learning, and renewal.

Those who do are likely to recognise that the role is not the end of a long career, but another beginning.

To grow into, and with their role, leaders need to create environments that feed their curiosity, challenge their orthodox beliefs, and fuel their continual learning and unlearning.

In his book, Spirit of Leadership, Dr. Myles Munroe says, "*the thinking of a leader (is what) separates him or her from the followers.*"

Scenario Planning is a good tool to anticipate

In 1965, Royal Dutch Shell started experimenting with a new way of looking into the future: scenario planning. Almost half a century later, scenario planning is still thriving at Shell and it has had a huge influence on how businesses, governments and other organisations think about and plan for the future.

Several principles have come to define the Shell approach. The most important is that scenarios are not predictions but plausible stories about the future. They are designed to help break the habit, ingrained in most corporate planning of assuming that the future will look much like the present. They create a safe space for dialogue and for acknowledging uncertainty – allowing an organisation to see realities that would otherwise be overlooked.

Credit: Living in the Futures: How scenario planning changed corporate strategy by Angela Wilkinson and Rolan Kupers, HBR Special Issue Summer 2020, original published May 2013

Other tools are, PESTLE and Force Field Analysis

Summary – Chapter 4

1   Apple and Samsung became phenomenally successful because they were driven by leaders with growth mindset.

2   Transformational leaders must think differently.

3   You must learn to anticipate change and crisis and plan.

4   Perspective and plans driven by boldness are required to live in the VUCA world and to survive the COVID – 19 fallouts.

Chapter 5

Adaptability (Attribute 3)

A daptability - the quality of being able to adjust to new conditions. **Adaptability** is required to solve *"problems for which there are no simple, painless solutions – problems that require us to learn new ways."* (Oxford English Dictionary)

The next quality is *Adaptability*. It is the ability to embrace change and adjust to new conditions. Famously, Kodak failed to see how the camera phone was impacting on their core.

"Adapting proactively. For evidence of how important it is for businesses and leaders to adjust to a rapidly changing environment, we need look no further than the aftermath of Brexit and the recent U.S. presidential election. Our analysis shows that CEO's who excel at adapting are 6.7 times more likely to succeed. CEO's themselves told us over and over that this skill was critical.

When asked what differentiates effective CEOs, Dominic Barton, global managing of McKinsey 7 Company, immediately offered: "It's dealing with situation that are not in the playbook. As a CEO you are constantly faced with situations where a playbook simply cannot exist. You're better be ready to adapt."

Credit: The Latest Research Leadership, Harvard Business Review, April 2020

It is interesting to note that Kodak sponsored the maiden edition of the FIFA U-17 soccer World Cup which held in Japan in 1985. Nigeria sensationally won that tournament. But the brand behind the event is no more on the scene.

Today's leader must be adaptable and flexible. Never take your success for granted and be ready to adapt if a change is coming. And it is the same in any business and any career.

Never take your success for granted and be ready to adapt if change is coming. And it is the same in any business and any career.

I will use three organisations to illustrate this point. **Encyclopaedia** Britannia believed it had an invincible worldwide niche. Sales in 1990 reached £650million. But when technological advances came along, they ignore them and failed to effectively adapt. By 1996, sales had dropped to $325million and Jacob Safra, a Swiss businessman was able to buy the company for a fraction of its book valued.

Similarly, **Polaroid** resisted technology's march. Sounding like the buggy whip manufacturer at the dawn of the automobile era, Polaroid CEO, Gary DiCamillo in a 1998 Harvard Business School profile said, "Some people think that photography is going to go away as everything in our industry becomes digitised. But I disagree. I think analogue photography will endure". Three years later, Polaroid filed for bankruptcy with nearly $1billion in debt.

Famously, **Kodak** failed to see how camera phone were impacting on their core. We all need to be adaptable, agile, flexible and in constant motion. Change has always been with us, but today the speed of change is greater than ever before. So, if you feel you are the market leader, and change is coming and you can't respond to the change easily, you will soon be out of business. So never take your success for granted. **(same as in page 60)**

Daniel Gilbert is the founder and chief executive of *Brainlabs,* a digital marketing agency, with offices in London, Austin, New York and Los Angeles. In an article *Adapt, or be crushed by the Fourth Industrial Revolution,* in **City AM**, a free business-focused newspaper distributed in and around London, England on Monday, October 9, 2017, Daniel wrote that *"No business has ever had the luxury of standing still. In the 1920s, American Express was founded as a delivery service (hence the name), and Marriott originally specialised in root beer rather than hotels. Any company that has survived this long has had to adapt to the immense changes of the twentieth and early twenty-first century, which is no mean feat. Still, as we approach a new era of technological and social transformation, defined by many as the 'Fourth Industrial Revolution', businesses will need to be more adaptable than ever before, if they wish to survive."*

Several examples abound of companies that fail to adapt. Daniel cited the example of Polaroid, highlighting the major reasons behind its collapse but attributing the main reason to *"be obstinacy within the leadership team about their business model. Instead of developing their software offering, Polaroid stuck rigidly to hardware (cameras) – and suffered immensely during the disruptive rise of mobile phone cameras."*

On the contrary, writes the author, *"As a counter-example, it's impossible not to think of **Amazon**. Jeff Bezos' insatiable appetite for new market expansion demonstrates remarkable adaptability. Love it or hate it, Amazon epitomises a business of the future: using automation, data, and adaptability to seize new opportunities (including, most recently, a first attempt at invading digital advertising).*

*The so-called super-platforms (**Amazon, Facebook, Google**),* *along with agencies like my own, are utilising the same technologies that will make or break businesses in any sector, given enough time. We are still at the early stages of a period of change that will be exponential, and, despite my own and many others' attempts, unpredictable.*

The only solution is to build a business that can continually be rebuilt. Greater adaptability is the most critical adaptation any business can make."

In an article in The Guardian titled, *'Nokia: the rise and fall of a mobile phone giant,'* it is said that *"From making rubber boots in a pulp mill to leading the world in mobile phones, Nokia failed to meet the challenge of the iPhone."*

Nokia is headed down the same path as Kodak. It hasn't risen to the market thrust of Samsung, which is threatening its brand leadership. It is a serious error to fail to adapt.

(Source: https://www.theguardian.com/technology/2013/sep/03/nokia-rise-fall-mobile-phone-giant, accessed on 04/01/18)

Be adaptable. Getting the most from life requires a flexible and intelligent approach. If a course of action doesn't work, you must be able to find effective alternatives. You must be able to adapt to change. Herbert Spencer said: *"Survival goes not necessarily to the most intelligent or the strongest of the species, but to the one that is most adaptable to change."*

Today's leader must be adaptable and flexible: and adaptive leadership is now a requirement for staying afloat in the VUCA world and the era of the Fourth Industrial Revolution. Many organisations and managers are struggling to stay afloat, entrepreneurially relevant and aligned in the volatile, uncertain, complex, and ambiguous nature of today's global business environment. The name of the game is turbulence. Turbulence, which connotes that, in both the academic and practical spheres, the rapid rate of change, is irrevocably swirling around many of us, tipping us this way and that, even as we attempt to navigate a safe passage through the chaos.

As an executive trainer, I have had the advantaged privilege of watching how companies and employees cope with the dynamism that defines today's world. I will attempt to illustrate this dynamism with my educated observations on how TWO different managers/leader tried to adjust to increasing turbulence in their company's business environment, with dramatically different results for them and their organisation.

Once more, let us do a quick overview of VUCA.

- *Volatility* — the nature, speed, volume, magnitude, and dynamics of change.

- *Uncertainty* — the lack of predictability of issues and events.

- *Complexity* — the confounding of issues and the chaos that surrounds any organisation.

- *Ambiguity* — the haziness of reality and the mixed meanings of conditions.

I will make the background of the two managers as lucid as possible. The two managers, Manager A and Manager B, work in a company that offers professional services to a market segment that has been increasing on a global scale. As the overall global business environment grows increasingly complex and competitive, many organisations of nearly all sizes have recognised the compelling need to avail themselves of this company's services. The wave of new regional and global players springing from emerging markets, which in the past had dismissed the need for such services, is now developing into a real growth market, with all the opportunities and challenges that inevitably accompany working with different cultural norms and, sometimes markedly different business models. After floundering about in a low-growth level for much of the 2000s, this service-providing organisation has seen double-digit growth in the last three years, as their customer base emerges from the recession and they now face even more significant growth and organisational challenges from the today's world.

However, it's not all a rosy picture for this company. This is because its particular market segment is very fragmented, with no primary provider accounting for over 5% of the market. It is also highly substitutable, with several types of providers ranging from the large and established, to small or one-offs. It is even more competitive, with new entrants from different sectors and emerging markets. The segment has not developed clear-cut, premium standards for what should ideally make up a high-quality customer experience.

Of further significance, the segment is a high-touch, relationship-oriented business which still suffers from a shortage of experienced professionals on both the provider and the buyer sides. Many players are still in a learning phase while seeking to professionalise, especially on the provider side, with their employees having to master multiple skills set rapidly to keep up with the steep and increasingly dynamic growth opportunities. In fact, like other fast-moving organisations trying to keep pace today, working in this company can only be characterised as being in a permanent stressful learning environment.

In response to these tendencies, the company's senior leadership changed a few years ago, with a new Chief Operating Officer, who is also chief executive of his unit, coming in from a much more established competitor. He came in with a blueprint that featured several critical changes to the fundamental business model, and an ambition to grow the business both financially and globally faster than had ever been experienced previously.

Finally, this service provider's overall holding company had, itself, been on a turbulent ride over the last decade, with several financial and organisational challenges at the macro level. Ultimately, all this have combined to produce a situation where the service provider has had to operate in an extremely "VUCA" organisational climate even while working with its clients' VUCA business environments. To express it for both good and bad, this company has been sailing on the very turbulent high seas almost continuously for several years, and, naturally, has many bruises to show for it. Many of its leaders have had little choice than to develop the adaptability that it takes to thrive in a VUCA world or move on.

Both leaders in my case study are managers of other executives, and who lead client-facing teams. Manager A is a seasoned field veteran who had joined the organisation in the mid-2000s, functioning as a team leader with responsibilities for business development, client management, and overall corporate delivery. His reputation for being a straight talker, a quick decision-maker, and for having a strong affinity for corporate profitability soon positioned him for a more senior role among his peers on the broader management team. Besides this, his ability to provide consistent clarity and direction continually emerged in his assessment reports, throwing him up as a charismatic team leader.

He always seemed to have a clear explanation for things, to ask the straightforward and undeniably pertinent questions of more senior managers when necessary, and to have an action-oriented disposition that focused his team firmly on results. The combination of these qualities reflected as this manager's ability to deliver above his target a few years ago and led the organisation to increase the size of his client base and to raise his salary accordingly. Without an iota of doubt, he appeared to be inevitably on his way to bigger things.

With the onset of the recession, the organisation's business environment, naturally, became increasingly turbulent, with some clients cancelling or postponing contracts. The new opportunities that presented themselves required more economical models. As for many companies, the business environment following the recession transformed into a new and normal dispensation that became increasingly reflective of the conditions of the VUCA world. This scenario was new and exciting, with challenging opportunities that combined with much more severe turbulence in terms of client expectations, pricing constraints, emerging competition, and greater complexity across the board for acquisition and delivery of services.

The company would have to stretch itself dramatically to adapt to these new and fluid market conditions, and that its leaders would need to pave the way by demonstrating an ability to adjust themselves. The new company, COO, was the embodiment of this style of leadership. Although he provided a vision, he empowered his managers to interpret it across their teams broadly. He also restructured the organisation to provide for increased collaboration, while encouraging competition, and he openly embraced the new complexity and ambiguity in the market.

During the COO's early months, Manager A emerged as being uneasily and quietly sceptical of the new strategic direction of the COO, and the organisation's perception of changes in the external business environment. Gradually, he started resisting the need to adapt, retreating instead to the apparent safety and comfort zone of tried-and-tested business models. He clung to past measures of success and failure, despite glaring evidence that some of these were no longer applicable in the new business milieu, or, worse, had become roadblocks to future growth. He refused to learn new skills, acting as if the new tools introduced by the COO were unnecessary even to target a new and more complex set of client opportunities that were presenting themselves.

Manager A, who was once open and accessible to many other employees in the company, compartmentalised them into "friends and foes," while steering his team in its direction within the larger organisation and actively discouraging collaboration. Seeing the world through a distinctly black-and-white lens that brooked no new perspectives, he argued that "ambiguity" was being used to mask problems that could be solved by bold, decisive leadership and that the real way to lead in the VUCA world was to 'draw some lines in the sand,' and stick to them. For this manager, what had once been conversations turned into one-way diatribes, as the manager seemed bent upon demonstrating that he had the answer for everything?

Despite attempts to mentor him, this manager, who has since moved on from the organisation became a lone oar rowing very hard the other way. For a time, his ability to focus attention on the company's legacy clients in the "tried and tested" business model helped meet revenue goals, but this only masked how failing to adapt to new skill sets, and more complex client situations, would eventually erode his team's top-line performance. His team members, initially energised by his precise, declarative, top-down leadership style, gradually became confused about direction and, eventually, they became disconnected from others in the company. The manager's sharp-edged, "us versus them" stance put most of the team in difficult and untenable situations, eventually causing many to become part of the "them". Finally, becoming isolated in his world, he stopped listening to anyone except the echoes provided by his close allies.

What is our analysis of Manager A? Was it just a question of a bad fit, which is what could happen in any organisation? The answer to this question will have to be "yes," However, from the broader perspective, the real issue was this manager's unwillingness to adapt to the increasing turbulence faced by his organisation. The key aspect was the product of a pervasive fear of failure, which undergirded the refusal to want to change, to try new approaches and learn new skills, and to accept that the world has become a much more turbulent, complicated place where some leadership styles were now outmoded. Was this manager self-aware? While it is a fact that his colleagues sensed some inner struggle on his part however, it would seem as if his ultimate point of self-reflection was to tell himself he was always right.

Now, let us contrast this man with another manager of men and resources at the same company, Manager B, whose essential ability and willingness to adapt has had a much different and more beneficial outcome for the organisation and its employees. This manager, who had garnered nearly ten years of management experience, was actually in a leading position in the organisation for several years before stepping aside four years ago to address specific, compelling, personal issues. When he came back, he had to make do with a lower-level management position. For some months, as expected, there was scepticism in the organisation that this "experiment" would work, and predictions that this person's ego or legacy from managing at a higher level would impede his work. There was also doubt that as a member of the 'old school,' he could "learn the new tricks" it would take to perform across the much more demanding level of skills that the organisation's new COO was demanding.

But, right from the outset, Manager B plunged into the world of adaptability. He re-tooled himself for a business model that required at least four times the skill set spectrum, and another four times control, compared with what got before his boss, the new COO had joined the company. It seemed like slow-going initially, mainly because of the drag coefficient associated with concerns about the manger's ability to "step down" from his previous role. However, this merely masked a determination by the manager to refit into the organisation and to leverage the new dynamics introduced by the COO as the vehicle.

So, what did this manager do to adapt to leading in a VUCA

world?

First, and perhaps most important to becoming an adaptive leader for turbulent times, he has let go of a lot of what defined success in his prior roles and organisational models, permanently shedding the impact of years of performance reinforcement and standards, while getting set to measure up to new ones.

Second, and related to the first, was an ability to curtail his ego, an enormously complicated challenge for a seasoned performer who had risen to higher heights only to have to shift backward.

A third was Manager B's keen desire to keep learning, and the ability to see the new leadership, and new organisation as an escalator to boarding the ship of a whole new set of skills.

A fourth was his commendable ability to adopt an "open-to-everyone-in-the-organisation" stance even to those who initially were doubters or detractors, and to new employees.

Finally, a fifth was his ability to work with the contradictions and paradoxes that increasingly come with navigating the VUCA world, rather than railing against them.

One thing is clear. We are moving from a world of problems, which demand speed, analysis, and elimination of uncertainty to solve, to a world of dilemmas, which require patience, sense-making, and engagement of uncertainty.

Therefore, to counter VUCA, we will require:

- **Vision** - an intent that seeks to create a future
- **Understanding** - the ability to stop, look, and listen
- **Clarity** - the ability to help make sense of the chaos.
- **Agility** - the ability to move with speed, fitness, and flexibility.

Perhaps these are traits of good leadership in any situation, not just for the VUCA world. This is valid. However, they are valuable in turbulent times, where so much of what is traditionally available for leaders to judge themselves is dangerously outmoded. Perhaps at the heart of Manager B's success in adapting has been his growing sense of self-awareness over the last several years. Known as someone who had carefully guarded his life and reactions, he took the opportunity of the position change and new organisational direction to re-examine his core values and re-align his career goals, shifting flexibly to accommodate himself within the unique perspectives that the increasing turbulence offered. Grounding one's self in who one is in this world and what one wants to stand for as a leader is also even more essential to leading in a VUCA world, where one's anchorage needs to be as steady as that of a ship in stormy waters.

So, what has resulted from Manager B's adaptation? Being able to let go of many past yardsticks of success has allowed this manager to be more open to new performance imperatives from both the client base and from within the company. While this manager still has some business growth goals to meet, he has re-oriented much of his portfolio growth strategy toward more complex and riskier, but more lucrative, potential client engagement, the kind that is the future of the business. He has also steadily embraced new performance measures by trying to put personal insecurities aside and bring humility to bear on his development. Similarly, his ability to embrace working with the contradictions and paradoxes that often accompany uncertainty and ambiguity has helped him keep his team fully engaged with organisational vision and strategy.

Keeping his ego in check in the face of an unusual career move, and showing a keen desire to keep learning, have both gradually earned him newfound respect from others in the organisation, a crucial characteristic for these VUCA times when employees are always looking for leaders who can acknowledge their imperfections and willingness to address them. Active learning has helped the manager acquire the new skill sets, and to be a role model, first for his team, and gradually for others. The ability to embrace learning, "un-learning," and "re-learning" is critical for leaders in the VUCA world, where many bodies of knowledge are changing so fast, with information and insight becoming irrelevant rather quickly.

Finally, this manager's ability to remain open and accommodating to everyone in the organisation, another practice that is grounded in humility and self-awareness, has resulted in the gradual gaining of trust and a spread of his influence with many employees, peers, and bosses. This, too, has been critically important to the organisation's overall leadership posture in VUCA times, as employees look for leaders to be available and to communicate often and honestly, as peers look to each other for ideas, support, and secure collaboration, and as senior leaders look for ideas, honest feedback, and clear input into, and loyalty toward, the vision, mission, and strategy.

However, this manager still has some distance yet to go in adapting his leadership for VUCA times, and he candidly admits this. Goals include further enhancement of some critical skill sets that permanently require facing up to longstanding insecurities about innate abilities, and continued shaping of his communication style toward more 'straight-shooting' and away from the 'sugar-coating' that has, in the past, left some to doubt the intent and value of his comments. Leaders who hold back out of fear, and whose words do not generate unassailable confidence are in danger of being relegated in these VUCA times.

Still, this manager has commendably made enormous strides toward adapting to VUCA times and is increasingly making a positive impact on his company's business and organisational culture, with the attendant personal rewards.

ADAPTABILITY AND THE US MILITARY

The US military, notably the Army, approached the Vietnam War with a conventional mindset, referred to as the 'Army concept.' The American method of counterinsurgency was 'almost a purely military approach,' which ignored political and social realities on the ground. Instead of focusing on protecting the Vietnamese people and denying the Communists a haven, the Army, in particular, believed that massive firepower was the best means to be 'utilised by the Army to achieve the desired end of the attrition strategy–the body count.' The American defeat was a 'failure of understanding and imagination.' The Vietnam War was fought from the Pentagon, and local commanders had no say in the matter. Even during the Iraq War, the Pentagon used a massive amount of data to analyse and direct the war.

Defence Secretary Rumsfeld's refusal to listen to men who were specialists in Middle East matters and understood the ground situation resulted from his denial of the reality that the United States was fighting an insurgency and not engaging in conventional warfare. Officers who believed that counterinsurgency strategy was to be employed, including General Petraeus, were transferred to insignificant postings and passed over for promotions. Therefore, officers stopped voicing their opposition to the views of Rumsfeld and his senior Pentagon officials. Strategic errors are common in war, and this wasn't just about going into Iraq with the wrong strategy. It was a failure; worse, a refusal to adapt.

The US Army's fortunes changed when Rumsfeld was removed because of heavy losses, and General Petraeus was made commander in Iraq. He brought back, with due promotions, those officers who were punished for airing contrary opinions and decision making was transferred to field commanders who knew the ground realities. An initial refusal to learn from what was going on and later the military's ability to learn and to adapt changed the tide of the war.

Unfortunately, in the other threats like Afghanistan, where the US is fighting a proxy war, it has not deployed the experience it had from the Iraq war. That is why the Taliban couldn't be defeated.

Change comes from a bottom-up approach. Good leadership is essential, but in a complex VUCA environment, it would be a mistake to lead through remote control.

Adapt early

Encyclopaedia Britannia believed it had an invincible worldwide niche. Sales in 1990 reached £650million. But when technological advances came along, they ignored them and failed to adapt effectively. By 1996, sales had dropped to $325million and Jacob Safra, a Swiss businessman, could buy the company for a fraction of its book value.

Similarly, Polaroid resisted technology's march. Sounding like the buggy whip manufacturer at the dawn of the automobile era, Polaroid CEO, Gary Dicamillo in a 1998 Harvard Business School profile said, "Some people think photography will go away as everything in our industry becomes digitised. But I disagree. I think analogue photography will endure". Three years later, Polaroid filed for bankruptcy with nearly $1billion in debt.

Famously, Kodak failed to see how the camera phone was impacting on their core. We all need to be adaptable and in constant motion. Change has always been with us, but today the speed of change is more significant than ever before. So, if you feel you are the market leader, and change is coming and you can't respond to the transition smoothly, you will soon be out of business. So never take your success for granted. *(same as in page 54)*

Survival of the fittest. Monday, April 3, 2017, City AM Ex-Dragon breathes fire over retail failures. Shruti Tripathi Chopra speaks to a retail tycoon about the sector's troubles.

In his view, retail failure is because of brands not adapting to changes. "There are always corrections, and heritage brands needs to change with the times. Consumer habits are changing so fast, so unless you invest in the business and consider the changing habits, you will lose your business and customers. You do have to be on your toes and reinvest in your business, and you have to have a vision," he says.

My mind went back to what had happened to the American car industry in the '70s, where leaders were over confident and lethargic in the face of competition from Japan. They hadn't taken sufficient notice of the changing environment, and by the time they did, it was too late to change their behaviour.

Again, the US watched as China offered American manufacturers a haven to produce cheaper products and export them back to the lucrative US market. Now, China's economic power has become a potent threat to the growth of America's economy. This has triggered Trump to launch a protracted economic war on China. How this turns out, remains to be seen.

Addressing the Challenges of Adaptability

The need for humans to adapt is not a new phenomenon, and those who point out that humankind has faced even more dramatic adaptation imperatives in the past are no doubt right. Having established that fact, we are where we are in the history of human development and the scope and pace of dynamic change in the marketplace and our organisations, and a failure to meet the challenges headlong will leave many companies behind and the human capital potential of their employees unfulfilled.

Globally focused companies and organisations from many

industries and fields of endeavour must help their leaders develop or further enhance their ability to adapt to the turbulent times. Leaders must become more comfortable and agile with ambiguous and contradictory demands, though focusing on managing paradoxes. There is an increasing need to focus on the skills and mindsets that it takes to move swiftly, and often without specific authority, in making fast decisions through influencing and networking. There is a need for speed, and for bringing all relevant resources to bear for impact in collaboration. There is a need to focus on self-awareness, reflection, and the need for quick recovery from failure. Above all, there is a need for leaders to embrace a mindset of change that is so critical in navigating the turbulent times of the VUCA world.

You must adapt your leadership style to accommodate and inspire the millennials

According to a recent interview with Richard Branson, he said, *"Ways of working and workplace culture have evolved, and millennials coming into the workplace have very different expectations from their job than previous generations. Younger employees don't see their roles as jobs for life and will leave a company if it doesn't match up to what they want.*

People are what have made Virgin what it is today, and my philosophy has always been treat staff how you would want to be treated. Train people, so they can leave, treat them well enough, so they don't want to.

Rigid corporate culture doesn't inspire people to think creatively and come up with innovative solutions. You get a lot more done when you get rid of the formalities and hierarchies. I may have been knighted, but I always prefer it when people call me Richard – leaders should be approachable and everyone should be treated the same. If you call your cleaner by their first name, then you should also do the same for your

CEO or founder.

It's not surprising that many companies are finding it challenging to adapt to our ever-changing world. Of the Fortune 500 companies of 60 years ago, only 12% make the list today and, in the UK, around 40 companies go into liquidation every day. The capability of their staff ultimately determines the ability of organisations to evolve successfully. Transformation of the organisation is inextricably linked to the transformation of individuals, and for that to be a reality, learning has to be at the core."

(Source: *The Future of Leadership: Rise of Automation, Robotics and Artificial Intelligence.* Brigette Tasha Hyacinth Monday, April 23, 2018)

We must adapt. Think of adaptability as a habit, something to practise. In the future, we will compete against mechanically enhanced workers who can work longer and harder than us—a new breed of elite super-workers emerges.

Robots will be in almost every sector. The idealised company for owners is one without employees. Robots can't get unionised or strike. They are a cost-effective and compliant workforce. They can work steadily, don't require breaks or vacations, sick leave, maternity leave, don't ask for raises, don't gossip or get disgruntled over missing a promotion, don't need weekends off, never leave the premises, don't lie, cheat, steal, antagonise, or complain. But coupled with AI, robots will be enabled and trusted to do much more.

According to PwC, these forces will cause four potential futures: one where humans come first, one where innovation rules, one where companies care, and one where corporate is king. Imagine what it will be like when you are no longer just competing for a job with another human. What will you think when your competition for a job is a smart machine with a serial number?

Despite the massive potentials of AI systems, they are still far from replacing many kinds of tasks that people are good at or tasks that require creativity, innovation, or empathy.

Individuals will have to grow in their lives and careers. If service jobs will become obsolete, then it's up to every individual to manage and transform themselves.

Become a better brand and a better version of yourself. While we have had robots, which have replaced minor jobs, we are still quite some time away from robots being so advanced that they can replace complex tasks such as persuading or negotiating. Communication, emotional and social intelligence, creativity, innovative thinking, empathy, critical thinking, collaboration, and cognitive flexibility will become the most sought-after abilities.

Regardless if you think AI is coming for your job or not, it's in your best interest to become a perpetual learner: Start by getting a high-level understanding of the changes coming from the Fourth Industrial Revolution, beyond AI, robots, and automation. Keep abreast of new developments and changes. This will help you not only to understand where risks to your career may come from but also identify opportunities for your future. Take a SWOT analysis. SWOT is the acronym for *strengths, weakness, opportunities,* and *threats.* Be sure to include not only your learned technical skills but also soft skills, interests and passions. Pay attention to tangential areas related to your career, not just to what is directly in front of you. Think of other areas where your skills can be applied. You will need to create every advantage to stay ahead. Consider alternative career paths and work on bridging the gap, think beyond your role.

Be a continuous learner, take classes online, volunteer, take part in discussions, and network. Keep learning. Keep growing. New technologies will create new opportunities in many fields.

There's an unprecedented shortage of programmers, data

scientists, cybersecurity experts and IT specialists, among others. For example, there's a 1 million shortage of skilled workers in the cybersecurity sector. **According to ISC2, that number will rise to 1.5 million by 2020**. A study of job ads from April found over 10,000 vacancies in the US for people with AI or machine-learning skills. Here's a selection of 10 occupations that weren't around in 2006: App developer, iOS developer, Android developer, Driverless car engineer, Cloud computing specialist, Big data analyst/data scientist, Sustainability manager, Drone operators. Digital marketing specialist, UI/UX designer.

Upwork, the largest freelancing website, released the 20 fastest-growing skills for freelancers in Q2 2017. The 20 fastest-growing freelance skills in Q2 2017 all experienced over 150% year-over-year growth, while the top ten grew over 300% compared to the same period last year (Q2 2016). 1) Virtual reality, 2) Natural language processing, 3)Econometrics, 4) Learning Management System (LMS), 5) Neural networks, 6) Penetration testing, 7) SEO auditing, 8) Image processing, 9) Asana work tracking, 10) Facebook API development, 11) Swift development, 12) Marketing analytics, 13) Geographic Information System (GIS), 14) Docker development, 15) Adobe Photoshop Lightroom, 16) Machine learning, 17) AngularJS development, 18) Video advertising, 19) Shopify development, and 20) Pardot marketing.

History has leveraged the productivity of everyone. AI will enormously leverage the productivity of those very few who can use creative and analytical thought to solve the problems of the rich. The rest will be surplus to requirements. It will destroy minimum wage jobs but will create more speciality jobs. Both the Canadian Government and the US Department of Commerce have authored reports suggesting that up to 40% of the tasks performed in our economies are in danger of automation within ten years.

This is a swift, substantial change that will merely leave some people behind. Not everybody is cut out to do technology work, and what about older workers? Some say that age discrimination is now taking place as young as 45, particularly in technology- and knowledge-driven fields. While every technological advancement in the past made multiple professions obsolete but created a more significant number of new jobs, this "knowledge revolution" is different.

Just look at the size of the most valuable companies in the world less than a generation ago. They employed millions or hundreds of thousands of workers. Look at the most useful companies today: Google is worth around $500B and has 72K employees. Facebook, with a value of approximately $350B, has 17K employees, and Waze was sold for $1.3B when it had 115 employees. This is a growing trend **where** we attribute ~~where~~ more and more value to less and fewer people. Most of US college graduates have a meaningless degree that will not land them a job, while the average student in the US has an outstanding debt of $35K ($1.2T total). This current knowledge revolution will necessitate fewer people with higher skills. This brave new world will demand initiative and entrepreneurship from everyone, while only a small portion of the population has the required spirit.

The fundamental mathematics of investment and finance require every company to pursue one central aim: Spend as little as you can to produce the most and the best output (products and services) that you can.

We've entered an era when computers can understand speech, respond to customer support questions, develop music, create unique art, and even generate new summaries and reports from data. Increasingly, we will struggle to distinguish between machine-generated and human-generated. Eventually, companies will have to disclose if a product is made by a human or machine — natural or artificial.

Products made by humans will be more expensive.

Companies will need to view future competitive advantage, processes, and organisation from a man-and-machine angle. Economic theory suggests that AI will substantially raise the value of human judgment.

Outsource or automate — whatever will reduce costs. So, take active steps to keep yourself relevant in the job market.

For example, between 31% and 50% of Kenya's GDP is estimated to flow through the mobile money service named M-Pesa.

Many companies back then thought the cell phone would just become a communication device. Instead, EDUCATION AI has the potential to change the delivery, quality, and nature of education.

Parents will need to teach their kids how to survive in the digital and the real world, and how to find the balance between the virtual and reality world to develop their social skills.

By 2020, the average person will have more conversations with bots than with their spouse. People will form relationships with artificial agents. We humans seem to want to maintain the illusion that the AI truly cares about us. This can work because, as a society, we have become disconnected. We prefer our technological gadgets for interacting with people. If we connect with people, it is on a superficial level. Today, many people are lonely.

In Britain and elsewhere, the subject of robots as potential life partners is coming up more and more. Some see robots as an answer for elderly individuals who outlive their spouses:

In the future, people will value their relationships with chatbots and robots more than human beings. They will grow attached to them and consider them as real persons.

Today, the eight wealthiest people on earth own as much wealth as the poorest 50% of the world. **The Economist** *highlighted the critical role of data in a cover story, in which it stated: "the world's most valuable resource is no longer oil, but data."*

Jack Ma, the founder of the Alibaba Group, stated that CEOs are soon to be replaced with AI. *"In 30 years, a robot will probably be on Time magazine as the best CEO,"* he said. Speaking at a China Entrepreneur Club conference, he warned that we should develop robotics to complement humans in the workplace and not as a replacement.

A recent McKinsey Global Institute report found that up to 25% of the work undertaken by a CEO could now be automated. *"We estimate that about 25% of CEOs' time is currently spent on activities that machines could do, such as analysing reports and data to inform decisions."* In the PwC Digital IQ Survey, 72% of business executives said they believe AI will provide the business advantage of the future. And 67% of executives expect AI to help humans and machines work together more effectively.

We will still require humans to do the jobs that require emotional intelligence, critical, and innovative thinking. These skills that a good CEO possesses cannot easily be substituted with a machine or robotic function. This means leaders will need to keep pace with advances in data analytics, Machine Learning (ML) and Artificial Intelligence (AI).

The most agile and adaptable companies and executives will thrive. Organisations that can rapidly sense and respond to opportunities will seize the advantage in the AI-enabled landscape. So, the successful strategy is to experiment and learn quickly. Over the next decade, AI won't replace CEOs, but CEOs who use AI will replace those who don't.

A company will assume the standards and ethics of its leaders. Therefore, having a business leader with a strong moral compass is essential for success. 'Ethics' comes from the Greek word '*Ethos*', which means 'custom' or 'habit'. Ethics is generally understood as ethical principles that govern a person's or group's behaviour. They are crucial to the way we live and work. They are our guiding principles as we relate to the world.

Ethical Leadership has been described by Theodore Roosevelt (leader, thinker and the 26th President of the USA) as "*having core values and the courage to act on them on behalf of the common good.*" The author also affirmed, "*To educate a man in mind and not in morals is to educate a menace to society.*" The financial crisis of 2007–2008 revealed there is a higher need for ethical leaders and transparency in business processes.

Ethical Leadership means: *Leading by example.* We can liken it to a parent/child relationship. You cannot set policies that employees need to live by and not live by them yourself. Standing up for what is right, keeping your word. Being reliable. Keeping promises, meeting crucial deadlines, and being there when people need you. Expressing concern for the common good. Being honest when no one is looking. Doing the honourable thing, even when no one, or even the structure is conjectured to check or stop you.

Agility

Speed, fitness, flexibility, agility. These are words more often used to describe a world-class athlete than an organisation or its leaders. By all empirical accounts, the 21st century is bringing a frenzy of innovation driven by the continuing digital revolution and expanding global markets. All relevant indicators show that the current environment of sped-up uncertainty, and change will not decrease.

Let us remember that the term VUCA describes the dynamic nature of our world today and has caught on in a variety of organisational settings to describe a business environment characterised, to so rehashing in different words, by

- **Volatility** — The nature, speed, volume, magnitude and dynamics of change;

- **Uncertainty** — The lack of predictability of issues and events;

- **Complexity** — The confounding of the problems and the chaos that surround any organisation; and

- **Ambiguity** — The haziness of reality and the mixed meanings of conditions.

Business leaders are struggling with how best to lead in a VUCA world. Most of the old rules do not apply now when people with connections matter at least as much or more than infrastructure. Boundaries around companies are shifting, forming global networks of complex stakeholder relationships. Gone are those days when a CEO has only one lever to pull to create and sustain organisational success.

For example, replacing less effective leadership talent with successful leaders from other organisations can help, but it is merely not sufficient. Slight levers must be pulled to create organisational congruence. Leaders can achieve the congruence needed to sustain success in a VUCA world only by making continuous shifts in people, processes, technology and structure. Leading this subtle and sophisticated dance requires the capability to sense and respond to changes in the business environment with actions that are focused, fast and flexible. This is what we mean when we attempt to describe leadership agility.

What Does Leadership Agility Look Like?

While few would argue about the need for greater leadership agility, few can articulate specific action plans for leaders to become more agile. Where do we begin? What levers hold the most promise for increasing agility in our leaders sustainably?

Let us brave the attempt to explore some specific requirements of agile leaders. These FOUR are not the full range of agile behaviours, but they are necessities in attaining agility.

1. Leaders must provide guidance and direction to teams working across time zones, cultures and organisational barriers.

   Leaders rarely work with team members on a face-to-face basis, forcing them to rely on a range of virtual communication channels. And team members come from a variety of disciplines, cultures and experience levels, making clarity of communication and mutual understanding an even more significant challenge. Effective leaders will learn to balance the requirements of task completion and relationship development with equal finesse.

2. Take more risks by briskly connecting talent and moving information and knowledge around the globe. It requires leaders to complement full-time employees with part-timers, consultants, suppliers and even customers, as part of the broader definition of the company's workforce. Effective and efficient talent management models enable high-performing companies to source, assess, assign and develop this mix of talent across various projects and initiatives. User-friendly technology supports these models and allows them to incorporate multiple sources of global information about the workforce into decision-making processes. A comprehensive learning management system helps support effective talent management.

3. Maintain a laser-like focus on employee commitment and engagement across generational, global, cultural and demographic boundaries. It is infinitely easy to lose the commitment of employees whose talent is most needed in times of uncertainty. A research conducted by The Centre for Work-Life Policy in the United States shows that employee

loyalty plunged from 95 to 39 percent from June 2007 to December 2008. With employees immersed in a sea of project and matrix relationships, a significant challenge lies in assigning accountability and focusing attention on strategic priorities.

Agile leaders learn to keep the balance between the right amount of delegation and the right amount of strategic direction, so teams of people can sense and respond to changing needs in their customer worlds. This means creating the environment for employees to develop improved work solutions and new products and processes, allowing needed decisions to come on more of a just-in-time basis, closer to the customer.

4.   Make collaboration among suppliers, partners, customers, part-time employees and consultants a signature part of organisational culture. Functional silos have no place in an agile organisation, and agile leaders regularly need to model collaborative behaviour. Agile leaders are learning how to infuse collaboration into work processes, job roles, and measures, rewards and development systems, thus generating changes in mindsets and behaviour. They need to identify the key customer/supplier relationships in which both sides enjoy collaborative innovation. It also can mean creating collaborative physical and virtual spaces that allow relevant stakeholders to have access to, post and comment on related ideas and materials.

A CASE STUDY

Developing Leadership Agility at A Consumer Products Company

This is how leaders at a consumer products company called Land O'Frost, in Lansing, Illinois, in the United States, are addressing the turbulence and uncertainty in their industry. In 2008, they assiduously began investing in creating agile leaders as a critical component of their competitive growth strategy for the next five years. Land O'Frost is a privately held maker and marketer of a product named "Great Tasting LunchmeatsTM," under the labels Premium, DeliShaved, Taste Escapes, Bistro Favourites, just to name a few. Land O'Frost-branded lunchmeat products rank third in market share in the highly competitive lunch-meat category, alongside products from much larger competitors Oscar Meyer from Kraft Foods, and Hillshire Farm from Sara Lee Corporation.

So, how can a mid-sized, privately held firm like Land O'Frost, sometimes referred to as LOF, compete with such mega brands in serving the needs of power retailers like Walmart, Kroger and the other major food retailers? When David Van Eekeren, the 38-year-old, third-generation Land O'Frost president, was asked this all-important question, this is what he had to say lucidly:

"It is all about great and safe products and a talented workforce led by agile leaders."

Recognising the importance of developing LOF's leadership talent to lead the enterprise into the next half-century, Van Eekeren knew it was time to invest in establishing a corporate human resources function. He hired Steve Sakats as the company's first vice president of Human Resources. Sakats brought perspective and experience in human capital development from *American Express*, *ARAMARK*, *Nabisco* and others, to help the LOF leadership team map a strong strategic commitment to future growth through leadership agility.

The Fall of the year 2008 brought a sudden and disarming economic crisis that crushed global confidence and paralyzed so many organisations and leaders. However, Van Eekeren was enthusiastic about pushing forward with creating an updated strategic plan that would capture and sharpen the vision, primarily through the development of leaders with agility at every level of the organisation. Beginning in October 2008 and into the first quarter 2009, the Land O'Frost leadership team worked together aggressively to build the first tier of a strategy map reflecting the vision for the future, that embraced an enterprise-wide focus on leadership and organisational agility.

Van Eekeren demonstrated his commitment to investing in building a leadership talent pipeline in February 2009 by bringing 75 key managers and sales team members of LOF to Chicago for a leadership development retreat. This had never been done before at Land O'Frost. The meeting enabled the leadership group of 75 to work cross-functionally to develop the new strategies and requirements for agile leaders.

This is what happened at that retreat

Small groups of six to eight participants discussed how to anchor shared leadership commitments to crucial business strategies. They did this by creating leadership agility competencies and metrics derived from key agility indicators. The key agility indicators aligned company objectives from sales, operations, finance, human resources and marketing. This work resulted in a very high shared leadership understanding of the keys to success for all parts of the enterprise and set up a very clear direction for continuous development and reinforcement of leadership agility.

Steve Sakats, the Human Resources leader at LOF, enumerated how creating agile leaders provided LOF with the following business results, and he is quoted below:

1. ***Anticipating Change and Initiate Action.*** *These were critical elements of our leadership, agility, capability-building initiative. Key leaders focused on monitoring the surge in commodity meat prices and adjusted our promotion strategy to reduce the impact of higher meat costs. That change would have taken considerably longer in the past, if it happened at all. We have been rewarded with sales velocity far greater than the industry.*

2. ***Generating confidence.*** *Our focus on leadership agility gave us the confidence to declare our intentions to be a growth-oriented company. Our first training session invited 75 employees. Our second training session increased the number of employees to 90 and included our sales brokers for over 140 participants. It was the first time we included both groups in any company function. The sense of the team and the commitment to our future have never been higher. The enthusiasm of our team is evident in our employee engagement results where our percentage of employees engaged is twice the norm for our usual survey. It provided a road map to success that everyone has rallied around. All associates know how we define success and how they play a specific role in contributing to that success.*

3. ***Liberating thinking.*** *The number of new product ideas and projects has ballooned. Also, our rigour and structure for a new product introduction have been dramatically improved. Our process leveraged new thinking about our commitment to technology, with LOF TV broadcasting in each facility, along with the introduction and use of emerging trends in corporate social networking. We created the LOF Agile Wiki: "A Virtual Corporate Meeting Place for Achieving Our Audacious Goals." The Wiki was designed to provide collaboration and an interactive platform to support our focus on an agile corporate strategy with postings of the strategy map, project status on all key initiatives and chat rooms to encourage idea generation to support innovation and employee*

engagement projects.

In summary, leadership agility is the capability of a leader to sense and respond to changes in the business environment dynamically with actions that are focused, fast and flexible. It is about a leader's ability to prepare all employees for a VUCA world in a way that enables them to shift their mindsets and supporting skills from *"I know change is coming, but I can't really see the potential changes that might impact our organisation"* to *"I see change coming, and I am prepared and already doing something about it."*

In a nutshell, we must anticipate.

Human resources can help increase leadership agility by:

- Understanding what it requires of leaders to survive and thrive in a VUCA world.

- Identifying their leadership agility strengths and development needs.

  Embedding leadership agility in their talent management processes.

Case Study on Speed and delivery efficiency: ZARA & H&M

Anyone who has shopped at Zara (or any of Amancio Ortega's eight brands) has contributed to Amancio Ortega's $67 billion retail empire. Ortega - the most prosperous retailer in the world, and the second-richest man in the world - also owns a host of other retail chains and brands: Pull&Bear, Massimo Dutti, Bershka, Stradivarius, Oysho, Zara Home and Uterqüe. His net worth climbed upwards to $2.5 billion since 2015 due to gains in the value of his extensive real estate holdings.

Inditex's super-efficient supply chain process delivers new designs in less than three weeks compared to the industry average of six months.

It does it at a lower cost than its competitors. Daniel Piette, fashion director at Louis Vuitton, notably described Zara as 'possibly the most innovative and devastating retailer in the world.'

Outside the high-end luxury segment, competition for the mass market is today fought on two levels: getting the basics at the right price and providing customers with the latest styles as quickly as possible. With the industry average design-to-store time of six months, Inditex and its main competitor, H&M, are pioneers of fast fashion, regularly achieving less than three weeks. More than anyone else, they have focused on getting the latest designs to their customers as quickly as possible. José Luis Nueno, professor of marketing at the IESE Business School in Barcelona and regarded as one of the world's leading experts on the retail industry, sees the Inditex approach as the role model for the future of retail: With the certainty that variety will lose out to speed and cost, we can foresee a world in which Zara and H&M are more successful than Gap and Neiman Marcus, and the Aldi model wins over the Wal-Mart one. Hypermarkets and department stores will lose out to discount stores and the speed merchants. This is clear. The shape of retailing has changed, and a clear-out of the also-rans will drive the consequences over the next decade.

And Professor Nueno highlights two key competencies as being critical – speed and scale: An essential capability for any manufacturer seeking a decent margin will be the ability to produce faster than the diffusion of a trend. The scale will dominate over choice. And these just happen to be what Inditex are good at. (Jones et al. (2012)

Summary – Chapter 5

1   Adaptability is essential for long-term survival. Kodak and Nokia didn't adapt and paid the severe price.

2   Samsung proves smart design and sleek technology are all you need to beat competitors.

3   Think differently and think well to stay ahead of the competition.

4   AI is great, but robots can't fully displace human effort.

Chapter 6

Accountability (Attribute 4)

Accountability — This is taken from The Book, Spirit of Leadership

"Authority is 20 percent given and 80 percent taken"

- *Peter Ueberroth*

The spirit of authentic leadership always possesses a sense of accountability and responsibility. True leaders readily embrace submission to authority and are conscious of their stewardship of the trust given to them by those whom they serve. The spirit of leadership seeks to be faithful to the sacred trust of the followers rather than doing what will please the leader.

In this chapter, I want to address a potential danger that leaders fall into and what we can do to prevent it. As I said earlier, the key to good leadership is the power to influence through inspiration, not manipulation. The danger of leadership is its potential for wielding power without answering to anyone else. Dictatorship and tyranny occur in the absence of a leader's submission to authority.

The protection of leadership, therefore, is in voluntary submission to a trusted authority. The spirit of accountability is the active manifestation of submission to authority.

THE SPIRIT OF LEADERSHIP

ACCOUNTABLE TO WHOM?

Let's begin by clarifying to whom the leader must be accountable:

1. Himself (his conscience)

2. The primary stakeholders

3. The general family of humanity

4. The Creator, as the ultimate authority

All true leaders are aware of their responsibility to a higher power. Particularly concerning the Creator, they know that they are accountable before God for their words and actions.

LEADERS AND ACCOUNTABILITY

A true leader knows always that he is not a law unto himself but should uphold established laws and treat others with respect as people made in the image and likeness of the Creator. He also listens to the advice and input of credible authority.

WHAT IS ACCOUNTABILITY?

In a nutshell, accountability is giving a reckoning for one's conduct and reporting on one's progress. It is also an admission of motives and reasons for taking specific actions.

THE ACCOUNTABLE LEADER

In Paul's letter to the people of Philippi, he explained that Jesus was willingly accountable to the Father when he was on earth.

ACCOUNTABILITY

Each of you should look not only to your interests but also to the attention of others. Your attitude should be the same as that of Christ Jesus: who, being in very nature God, did not consider equality with God something to be grasped, but made himself nothing, taking the very nature of a servant, being made in human likeness.

Jesus continually referred to his accountability to the Father, making statements such as *"My food, is to do the will of him who sent me and to finish his work"* and acknowledging the Father's affirmation of his leadership: *"The very work that the Father has given me to finish, and which I am doing, testifies that the Father has sent me."*

"On [the Son of Man] God the Father has placed his seal of approval." In developing the spirit of accountability, we can have no better example than his.

Of course, there are other examples of individuals outside of the Christian community, who have given us good examples of stewardship. However, the principles remain the same, whatever your religious persuasion. Transparency is vital.

HOW TO BE ACCOUNTABLE

The following are some guidelines for incorporating accountability into your life:

- Commit yourself to be accountable to your convictions.
- Establish the Word of God as your final judge and authority.

- Appoint and submit to a group of tested, respected, credible, and mature people for advice, correction, criticism, and instruction. A true leader knows always that he is not a law unto himself.

- Choose friends who are committed to the high standards of the Word of God and give them the right to judge you by it. Perhaps the best advice for being accountable is the following, which Paul wrote to the first-century church at Colossae:

"Whatever you do, work at it with all your heart, as working for the Lord, not for men, since you know that you will receive an inheritance from the Lord as a reward. It is the Lord Christ you are serving." (Colossians 3; 23-24)

To manifest the leadership spirit hidden within you, you must embrace the attitude of accountability. Always be conscious you are responsible for those below and above you in everything you say and do. Know that whatever you do as a leader may be personal, but it is never private. Your ultimate accountability is to the Creator of all leaders, who knows the thoughts and attitudes of your heart.

ACCOUNTABILITY

What does accountability look like in today's world? How does accountability in a particular world differ from accountability in an uncertain one?

Within the context of VUCA and the Fourth Industrial Revolution, it can no longer be that we just follow the plan as initially set, since it needs to change in response to changing conditions, new information, and lessons learned. So, accountability will be a vision of where we want to get to, and not the "how to get there" plan. Again, this means we are tracking indices that we can't measure, as no qualitative data is available, and we don't know the steps that will need to be taken to achieve the desired results. However, we can monitor whether we're moving closer to, or further away from, our vision. This also means that we need to acknowledge proactive behaviour, which means doing what needs to be done now, not waiting to be told, a feat that may require a culture shift. From a leader's perspective, this isn't the most common level of delegation and, again, it needs to be negotiated and monitored with care. And this, too, takes a different set of leadership characteristics and skills.

Accountability has become a leadership swan song over the past decade. It is often used but vaguely defined. Many leaders, in attempting to unravel the true connotation of accountability, would typify it as "ensuring that you stay true to your principles," or "finding a place where you're true to yourself." Even those who won't talk explicitly about authenticity or purpose tend to fall back on leadership qualities; they consider essential: integrity, honesty, personal values, self-awareness, and trustworthiness. To some extent, pragmatism should lead us to embrace accountability as a response to the heightened visibility and transparency requirements that leaders face. You can't have a hidden side and a real side.

Broadly, however, since trust typically follows in the wake of transparency, we must view accountability as critical, both outside and inside the organisation, for the former to generate trust among a full group of stakeholders, and for the latter, as a cornerstone of productive collaboration that requires leaders to have a high level of trust from colleagues that he will do the right thing. Accountability is the fuel that drives trust.

Yet to be an accountable leader is no mean task. Stakeholders view trust and transparency as commitments to stability. As one corporate leader once said, "trust is created by a promise, and maintained by meeting that promise repeatedly." This makes it difficult for leaders to adapt to new challenges, as the new behaviours leaders used to meet these challenges stand the genuine risk of being perceived by stakeholders as contradictory. Such perceptions risk destabilising a leader's claims to accountability and authenticity and thus squandering the trust he has built up. Essentially, what this translates to is that an ever-widening group of stakeholders with competing demands will require different behaviours, and leaders will increasingly face some version of this 'authenticity–adaptability' paradox.

What differentiates leaders who feel successfully accountable and authentic from those who have difficulty remaining true to themselves? The valid response to this will have to be an overriding sense of purpose. As another corporate leader once said, "if you suddenly start losing focus on what your sense of purpose was at the outset and start becoming 'everything to everyone,' it usually is the beginning of the end."

This view leads us to a more precise definition of accountability: being true to personal purpose. However, another problem arises when the need to adapt to conflicts with a leader's sense of purpose. This is most likely when leaders, to keep pace with change, indiscriminately adapt themselves to new demands. The effect can be analogous to cutting the anchor line of a boat, thus putting executives at the risk of losing sight of their fundamental values and goals. Human resource issues represent a typical example of how a leader's index of accountability can be called to question. People decisions are often the healthiest choices leaders face. A familiar story is when a leader needs to fire an executive who is both high-performing and a friend to him because the executive had violated the company's ethics code. A leader once admitted, "I felt strongly supportive of the executive, but not to take any action would have confirmed everybody's view, internally and externally, that I was without moral fibre."

A publication launched in Davos at the World Economic Forum 2015 offers a useful insight into how CEOs experience the changing nature of their role and turn their new challenges into opportunities for business and personal growth. According to 'The CEO Report: embracing the paradoxes of leadership and the Power of Doubt', a genuinely accountable leader must have a sense of purpose that is true and genuine.

A corporate leader once had an awkward conversation with an employee who had just been laid off. Although this leader expected a furious reaction, he was surprised instead to find grudging acceptance. The employee said, "Although I'm personally devastated, we all respect you for taking a decision which needed taking, and perhaps if it were taken a couple of years ago, we wouldn't be in this mess." The lesson the leader in reference drew from these gets to the heart of the accountability challenge. Almost by definition, you only get the decision that either nobody else will make, or nobody else can make. And the scariest thing, for someone working in a business, is seeing with clarity that change needs to happen and seeing that their leaders are either unwilling or unable to make those decisions. That's a terrifying ship to be on.

What is the solution to ethical dilemmas such as these? leaders can only feel most comfortable when their sense of purpose is aligned with that of the organisation. A leader must be unequivocal about what his personal goals are and make sure his motivations are aligned and compatible with the organisation and where it's going. By prioritising their roles as responsible and accountable stewards of the business leaders will find alignment between the organisational needs and their purpose. When the personal and corporate purpose is aligned, it can guide organisational relationships and drive decision making, even when the decisions raise uncomfortable contradictions. Defining and aligning purpose, therefore, becomes the touchstone for reducing doubt around tough decisions that can easily task a leader's index of accountability.

Some tough decisions pose a moral dilemma. In that situation, a leader should do what's imperative, after looking at the bigger picture. According to Lincoln, "No life is ever taken to save an arm, but the arm is often severed to save a life". That's the reality that should guide hard choices.

Resilience is essential for an excellent leader to sustain genuine accountability, and nurturing personal resilience is a skill leaders must develop over time, and they need energy, courage, and strength as coping mechanisms for the physical, emotional, and intellectual demands of their jobs.

Once leaders can verify that they align their decisions with their values, there is less regret. Good leaders should ensure that their decisions are supported by both the factual information they gather, and the personal values they hold. Ultimately, the accountability-adaptability balancing act is the master paradox, and only by first being sure of their purpose and authenticity can they hope to later steer their way through the many other paradoxes the role introduces as they cope with individual decisions.

Ethical leadership is fast becoming synonymous with accountable leadership. It was John Maxwell who said, "*Doing the right thing may not always be easy…, but it is always right.*" Truly, the world is in an ethical dilemma. We can define an ethical dilemma as an undesirable or unpleasant choice relating to a moral principle or practice. When we find ourselves in such situations, what do we do? Do we toe the easy path, or do we do the right thing? Often, a convenient lie can easily conceal an error. Do we tell that lie? The prospective client appears vulnerable. Do I coat my proposal to him in such a way that he finds my service to him irresistible, even though I'm aware that I do not possess sufficient competence to give him optimal service? The sales clerk has given me too much change? What should I do?

According to John Maxwell, one of the world's leading experts on Leadership, when people make unethical choices, it is usually for three reasons.

The first is that people do what is most convenient.

The second reason is that people, almost invariably, will do whatever it takes to win. Most people hate losing. Businessmen and women, in particular, crave the thrill of winning through achievement and success. The critical and perhaps flawed concept is that they think they must juggle two choices: being ethical and winning. The story is famously told of a senior executive of a leading company in the United States who, at a preliminary brainstorming session for an upcoming national sales conference, enthusiastically suggested the presentation of a paper on ethics. A previously noisy room suddenly went silent as, an awkward moment later, discussion resumed as if the hapless executive had never uttered a word. She let the matter drop but took it up again with her CEO when she ran into him later in the day.

Fully expecting his support for what she considered a great idea, she was taken aback when he said, while admittedly, the question of ethics was an important issue. There was still a place and time for everything. He would prefer an upbeat and motivational sales meeting. He felt ethics was a slightly negative subject! This opinion, without doubt, is shared by many business people, who labour under the belief that ethics can only constrain their options and opportunities, truncating their potential for business success. Agreeing with Henry Adams, a Harvard history teacher, who said: "Morality is a private and costly luxury," they seem to echo the old refrain: the excellent guys finish last!

Often, people find themselves presented with only two choices: to succeed by doing whatever it requires, even if it is unethical; and to subscribe to ethical conduct and lose. This can be a genuine moral dilemma. The simple fact is: few people set out with a dishonest mindset, but the equally irrefutable fact is that even fewer people desire to lose.

The third reason people make wrong choices is that people would rather deal with their ethical difficulty by deciding to do what they perceive to be right in that moment, by the prevailing circumstances. People set their standards right being determined by the situation. This form of situational ethics has resulted in chaos, with standards that can change from situation to situation. To further bolster this point is a course that is offered at the University of Michigan in the United States, 'The Ethics of Corporate Management', whose prospectus states: "This course is not concerned with the personal moral issues of honesty and truthfulness.

It is assumed that the students at this university have already formed their standards on these issues." To make matters worse, people have a natural inclination to be lenient with themselves, generally judging themselves according to their good intentions, while, however, setting much higher standards for others and judging them by their worst actions. It would appear, therefore, that, while in the past, decisions were based on ethics, ethics are now based on choices.

Fortunately, there seems to be an increasing universal desire for ethical dealing in business. Companies are witnessing a renaissance, as the realities of the times, while still asking for critical executives who can make more money for their companies, and always take tough decisions, yet demand a more substantial need for integrity and the setting of more realistic, even if conservative corporate goals.

The conclusion of any right-thinking businessperson must be that it is possible to do what is right and still succeed, even superlatively, in business. It has been discovered that companies that are dedicated to doing the right thing and insist on a written commitment to social responsibility, and consistently act on it, are much more profitable than those who do not.

In the political spectrum, the electorate is also demanding proper accountability from their leaders and accountability is also one of the core tenets of good governance.

In a culture of accountability, you must make time to reflect on the state of leadership accountability within your organisation. So, how can we drive a culture of accountable leadership into our organisations? A study by the Institute for Corporate Productivity, titled Creating a High-Performance Culture, suggests that encouraging self-awareness and… Some highlights have been hidden or truncated because of export limits.

From the top and not followed by a company's leaders, which is what occurred with the ethics policies that Enron, Citigroup, Wells Fargo, and countless others proclaimed they had. Model the behaviour you want others to follow. Today's organisations want leadership accountability not just in the present but in the decades that follow. Some of the best leaders are the ones most respected in their industry. They are known to serve, develop others, and are authentic. While they hold others accountable, they allow themselves to be held to the same standard, and sometimes even a higher one. Set clear goals and expectations. You can't create a culture of accountability unless you first clarify expectations and authority. Our first step to creating a culture of accountability is to define precise results within the organisation. Some highlights have been hidden, or truncated, because of export limits.

Holding people accountable

An article in the Harvard Business Review by Darren Overfield and Rob Kaiser (2012) highlighted thus: "*By far and away the single-most shirked responsibility of executives is holding people accountable. No matter how tough a game they may talk about performance when it comes to holding people's feet to the fire, leaders step back from the heat.*" Accountability of people at all levels is vital for any organisation to be successful. The best way to hold everyone accountable is through mutual respect and leading by example from the top down. It takes a strong leader not only to hold themselves responsible but to hold others. We need always to hold each other responsible. Unfortunately, most employees view accountability as something that happens when performance declines problems... Some highlights have been hidden or truncated because of export limits.

Were my actions in line with my values? What could I have done differently today? As a leader, one of your most important jobs is to communicate the business core values, so they serve as the moral compass for the organisation. Make sure you are also following those values. Know what you stand for and never compromise principles. If something has gone wrong, and you were responsible, you need to take ownership and sincerely apologise. Be honest. When people lie, they cannot be accountable. Absence of accountability leads to chaos, and then anything goes.

Could I have done anything differently today? As a leader, one of your most important jobs is to communicate the business core values, so they serve as the moral compass for the organisation. Make sure you are also following those values. Know what you stand for and never compromise principles. If something has gone wrong, and you were responsible, you need to take ownership and sincerely apologise. Be honest. When people lie, they cannot be accountable. Absence of accountability leads to chaos, and then anything goes.

Have a person who will hold you accountable. A friend, co-worker, or a family member. Someone who will be honest with you. Or have a leader whose qualities you would like to emulate. In building our leadership lives, we enjoy looking at some role models who are a good example. Remember, no one is perfect. People make mistakes. But we need a model; someone who personifies the goals we have set for ourselves, who has travelled the path before us, and to whom we can look for wise counsel. As we dedicate and submit ourselves to service, we must be changed into the image of true leadership. For example, my role model for ethical and servant leadership is Jesus Christ. Usually, when I ask students in my presentations at schools, who are their role models, many name politicians or celebrities of questionable character. Most don't see lying as bad if it doesn't physically hurt anyone.

If these are our future leaders and they accept poor behaviour as the norm, then what will leadership look like? As a society, we need to place a higher metric on ethical behaviour when electing leaders. Find activities that can keep you on the right path. For me, it's sermons. This keeps my moral compass grounded. I never get complacent and feel I am perfect. You always must keep working on yourself. All of us are bombarded with the thinking of others. The news is just full of politics and adverse events. There is so much noise around which can cloud your reasoning. For me, it's refreshing to tune out and take in God's Word. It is spiritually uplifting, plus it reminds a leader we are part of something much bigger than our ambitions.

The essence of accountability is further stressed in a leadership development article by Laci Loew, the Vice President and Principal Analyst, Talent Management Practice, Brandon Hall Group.

In *'The Buck Stops Here: A Culture of Accountability Drives Effective Leadership'* (2014), Loew stressed "*In Brandon Hall Group's 2014 State of Performance Management Survey, 34% of global organisations said that executives do not hold leaders accountable for performance. In our 2014 State of Talent Management Survey, results showed that 39% plan to increase or significantly increase their focus next year on holding managers accountable.*

Without accountability, even the most brilliant, hard-working, well-intentioned leaders fail. They fail to meet their performance goals, they cannot develop their teams; they fail to hire top talent; they cannot coach their employees; they cannot communicate; they cannot optimise performance, and they fail the business overall. Effective leadership requires real accountability."

Essentially, Loew described accountability as leadership standing up to own the outcomes of their decisions for team and for the organisation and not apportioning the blame for inadequacies or unfavourable outcomes to their colleagues or subordinates. They also seek to make things right when the undesirable outcomes show up. Accountable leaders question the decisions and processes that shape your organisation. They ask questions, and they find answers — the best solutions.

A good leader must realise that if things go right, he should share the credit; if they go wrong, he ought to take the blame because the responsibility, for leadership fall squarely on the leader.

President Harry Truman of the United States of America famously known for assuming accountability for the performance of his administration was said to have had a plaque at his desk, displaying '*The Buck Stops Here*'!

Summarily, Loew's suggested strategies for leaders to become more accountable are fourfold:

- Honesty – setting aside personal pride and an admittance of mistakes where such abounds

- Genuine and voluntary display of humility – accountable leaders say "I'm sorry" when the needs arise and seek to make corrections alongside

- Accountable leaders seek inputs from colleagues, including bosses, peers, friends and partners

- They are also able to assume responsibility – taking on challenging tasks, not shirking in their duties of leadership and functional contributions.

Source: http://www.brandonhall.com/blogs/the-buck-stops-here-a-culture-of-accountability-drives-effective-leadership/ accessed Monday 13 April 2020

Summary – Chapter 6

1   Accountability gives credibility to leadership.

2   Trust weighs heavily on accountable and transparent leadership.

3   Ethical morality cannot be divorced from true leadership.

Chapter 7

Inspirational (Attribute 5)

E motional Intelligence (EQ) is the ability to perceive, control and evaluate emotions – it therefore involves perceiving, understanding and regulating emotions. Researchers credit Daniel Goleman as having made the term popular with his broad-based works in 1995, however Michael Beldoch, a psychologist at Cornell University, was first reputed to have referenced the term in 1964.

(Source: *Emotional Intelligence: What is it, interpretation models and controversies.* https://blog.cognifit.com/emotional-intelligence/ accessed Sunday 12 April 2020)

Daniel Goleman however explains the concept of inspirational leadership in his Emotional Intelligence Model, where we are told to start our leadership journey by becoming self-aware, as we need to do this before we can manage ourselves. We then need to understand others before we can manage others. Starting with our behaviour and self-awareness is the key.

Goleman stated that the most effective leaders use a range of styles and adapt their style to suit the situation. To lead in the VUCA World and the 4th Industrial Revolution, you must be able to inspire everyone to act.

The Essence of Inspirational Leadership

Lucy Finney succinctly highlighted the subject of inspirational leadership in the white paper, '*Inspirational Leadership: Six Must-Haves to develop inspirational talents within your organisation.*' An Inspirational leader is a role model guided by a set of morally sound core values. He/she behaves in a way that is aligned with the organisation's values and conducts his/her work in a responsible and accountable way. Such leaders continuously work to improve their leadership skills and deliver high standards of performance. They are authentic leaders who 'walk the talk' and inspire others to follow and raise their performance level to achieve more significant outcomes.

I should think of inspirational leadership as a leadership ethos that creates a climate where teams and individuals flourish. The climate people work in stimulates aligned action towards successful outcomes, people feel empowered, teaming is visible, enthusiasm is present, and individuals are committed to the success of the organisation.

In the past, leaders like Prime Minister Winston Churchill and President Franklin Roosevelt provided inspirational leadership during the Second World War. US President, John Kennedy did the same during the turbulent 60's. New Zealand Prime Minister is considered the most effective leader in the world, because of her focus on empathy and her proficient handling of the fearsome COVID – 19 Pandemic.

(Credit: https://www.apm.org.uk/media/12077/thales-whitepaper_inspirational-leadership.pdf accessed Saturday 18 April 2020)

John Adair's Action-Centred Leadership

The Action-Centre Leadership concept is that leadership is about getting everyone to act. John Adair is a leading proponent of this model. Adair's Action-Centred Leadership offers a functional blueprint for leadership and it is applicable to all strands of management.

It advocates that good managers and leaders should be in command of the three main areas of an action-centred leadership, using these singly and jointly according to rising demands and situations.

John Adair's Action-Centred Leadership model centres on the following responsibilities and illustrated with his iconic 'three circles' diagram as in below.

• Achieving the task

• Managing the team or group

• Managing individuals

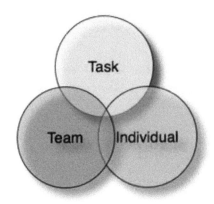

(Source: https://www.businessballs.com/leadership-models/action-centred-leadership-john-adair/ accessed Saturday 18 April 2020)

John Adair has been described by Sir John Harvey-Jones as, "without doubt, one of the foremost thinkers on leadership in the world."

So, who is John Adair?

After graduating from Cambridge University, Adair was commissioned into the Scots Guards. He later became a senior lecturer in military history and adviser in leadership training at the Royal Military Academy in Sandhurst. In 1979, he was appointed the world's first Professor of Leadership Studies at the University of Surrey.

As a (now) Visiting Lecturer in Leadership at the University of Westminster, I have always looked up to - and followed - John Adair. He was the leading thinker who first awoke in me a passion for leadership.

His model, Action-Centred Leadership, and the simple, practical and easy-to-grasp thinking behind it, gave me the hope that I could be a good leader. It then gave me the tools to start my leadership journey and stood me in good stead when I studied other leadership theories.

Today I still refer to John Adair's work in many of my leadership development programmes. I have seen so many others recognise its value. They just seem to get it. But what is "it"?

Action-Centred Leadership

In any situation where a group of people are trying to achieve some goal, one or more of those people will emerge and act as a leader to the others.

Look again at this sentence more carefully. Break it down into elements. What are they?

According to John Adair, there are three elements to all leadership situations. They are:

The achievement of a goal or task. This may be the completion of productive activity, or it may be a less tangible goal. We know that active groups have clear goals shared by all members. Often the task brings the group together.

The group of people performing the task. It is likely that the task will only be achieved if all members of the group work together to the common good. Therefore, the group itself must be understood as an entity in its own right.

Each member of the group involved in the task. While the group will take on a life of its own, individuals do not lose their own identity. Their needs as people must continue to be met if their allegiance to the group, and their motivation to achieve the task, is to be sustained.

This approach, 'Action-Centred Leadership', is centred on the actions of the leader. The leader must balance the needs of each of the three elements. The effective leader is the one who keeps all three in balance; that is who attends to all three at the same time. If any one component is ignored, the others are unlikely to succeed.

The three elements can conflict with each other. For example, pressure on time and resources often increases pressure on a group to concentrate on the task, to the detriment of the people involved. But if the group and individual needs are forgotten, much of the effort spent may be misdirected.

In another example, taking time creating a good team spirit without applying effort to the task is likely to mean that the team will lose its focus through a lack of achievement.

An approach that a skilled leader might take in any challenge is to balance the needs of all three elements:

- *Identify and evaluate the task.*

- *Communicate these to the group and gain their commitment.*

- *Plan the achievement of the task with the group.*

- *Identify resources within the group and allocate responsibility to individuals.*

- *Monitor and evaluate the progress of the whole group and individual members.*

- *Communicate feedback to the group and support, praise, and encourage individuals.*

- *Review plans and make changes with the group until the task is achieved.*

John Adair is one writer who has created his list of what leaders do. His list is linked into his Action-Centred Leadership model, which uses the headings of "Task", "Group" and "Individual".

I suggest readers should have a look at John Adair's website (www.johnadair.co.uk) to learn more about the man and his work.

Vision Articulation: A vision is what an organisation wishes to be like in some years in time. A mental picture of the future. It is a constant force and a critical anchor that drives decisions, actions, and judgments.

"Good business leaders create a vision, articulate the vision, passionately own the vision, and relentlessly drive it to completion." (Jack Welch, former CEO, GE).

In his book, Leading Change, John P Kotter, said, "*Great visions are nothing if they cannot be communicated. Thus, the use of story/metaphor, multiple media (people), simplicity and repetition, and leading by example all apply.*"

A vision is what an organisation wishes to be like in some years' time. A mental picture of the future. It is a constant force and a critical anchor that drives decisions, actions and judgments.

ENFORCERS OF CHANGE

Dubai, in the United Arab Emirates, used to be a desert, covered with (sand) dunes. Its seaport, having been in operation from the days of the Arabian tales, was limited in its scope, capacity and output. Kings came and left. Kingdoms conquered and changed the horizon several times. The British, too, were involved. However, the most considerable change to Dubai was with Sheik Maktoum who saw the possibilities of this desert island becoming the playground of the world, the greatest trade zone of the Middle East, and a place where architectural feats would meet with a global display of wealth. The rest is history. Not only did Sheik Maktoum see this vision, but he also enforced it and challenged those who followed him to see the same and make it happen.

The second enforcer of change who comes to mind is Margaret Thatcher, Prime Minister of Great Britain from 1979 to 1990. Margaret Thatcher did not allow her femininity to stop her from advancing substantial policy changes that were to change the trajectory of the whole country. First, she took on the labour union who, until she became Prime Minister, had great powers which brought most governments to their knees. However, having picked on the miners during a significant and long strike, she enforced policies that turned the country around. Mrs Thatcher also redirected the focus of the country to become more Eurocentric than its previous involvement with the various nations that made up the British Commonwealth of Nations. She felt that it was more beneficial to the country she ruled, to focus on Europe than those nations.

The first things are the vision.

- **Vision:** leaders provide direction and have a clear picture of the picture

- **Inspiration:** Leaders inspire people to work towards the image and often act as role models and led by examples

- **Reaction to change:** most leadership relates to instigating or reacting to change; good leaders are therefore persistent and do not give up at the first obstacle.

Vision articulation

- Effective and clear communication is a critical element to inspire others.

- Watch how you speak, and what you say as you are inspiring people to follow.

- Listen, show interest and enthusiasm.

- Ability to communicate a compelling strategic direction, vision and values to all stakeholders across various mediums

- When working with a global workforce, leaders will need the ability to communicate effectively across cultures. Like a location pointer on a GPS map, leaders must clarify the current situation concerning changing external demands continually. Equally crucial for leaders is to reiterate and reinforce vision, values and strategies. Finally, leaders must help others in clarifying the meaning of their work, communication and clarity being the currencies of effective leadership.

- Do you have that? So, when people are going into leadership positions, they need vision; they must be able to articulate that vision.

- When they can do that, followers will follow them. Steve Jobs could convince the Chief Executive of Pepsi to leave that company and join Apple. How was he able to do that? He could sell the vision. Jobs convinced John Sculley to let go of Pepsi with the famous line: *"Do you want to sell sugar water for the rest of your life or do you want to come with me and change the world?"*

- Ability to communicate ideas to people of different cultural and educational background, to "read people" from a diversity of experiences

- Ability to communicate them to all stakeholders across various medium

- Ability to delivering a compelling strategic direction, vision and values and build the capability and capacity of employees

KISS APPROACH

*KISS, a design principle noted by the U.S. Navy in 1960, stands for "**keep it simple and straightforward**." You may have heard some of the other variations to the acronym, including "**Keep it short or simple**," and "**Keep it simple, stupid**.**

(Source: *"Keep It Simple: Why Businesses Need to KISS More and How to Do It"* by Danny Mola, business.com member, July 28 2016 https://www.business.com/articles/keep-it-simple-why-businesses-need-to-kiss-more-and-how-to-do-it/ accessed Monday 21 December 2020 19:25hrs)

At its most basic, KISS reaffirms simplicity as a key ingredient in instilling understanding and a smooth flow of information from the initiator to the target audience and vice versa.

In 2010, Jobs introduced the first iPad with a slide showing the new tablet as a "third device" between a smartphone and a laptop. The iPad, he told the audience, would also come in "three models": 16, 32, and 64 GB of flash storage.

Try to apply the Rule of 3. Divide a presentation into three parts. Introduce a product with three benefits. Give me three reasons to hire you! The rule of 3 – It worked for Jefferson, it worked for Jobs, and it will work for you.

Tip #1:   Slice the Speech/presentation/communication into Groups of Three. Dale Carnegie said, *"Tell them what you will tell them, tell them, then tell them what you just told them."*

Tip #2   Use a Three-Part Organization Structure

Tip #3   Use the Rule of Three for Phrases, Sentences, and Words

Making people understand and live for the purpose of your organisation

- Start with WHY?

- Articulate the purpose to them

- If they buy into it, they will live it.

Examples of companies with the dominant purpose

- "Nourishing families so they can flourish and thrive." – **Kellogg's**

- "To help people manage risk and recover from the hardship of unexpected loss." – **International Airlines Group**

- "To put a smile on the face of everyone we touch." – **Nintendo**

- "To create a better everyday life for the many people." – **IKEA**

- "To bring inspiration and innovation to every athlete in the world." – **Nike**

- "To inspire and nurture the human spirit – one person, one cup and one neighbour at a time." – Starbucks

- "To refresh the world in mind, body and spirit. To inspire moments of optimism and happiness through our brands and actions. To create value and make a difference. – **Coca-Cola**.

- "To embrace the human spirit and let it fly" – **Virgin Atlantic**

- "To help people all over the world make progress in their lives through learning." – **Pearson**

- "To inspire and develop children to think creatively, reason systematically and release their potential to shape their own future, experiencing the endless human possibility" – **Lego**

- "To achieve the best outcome for the pensioners on whose behalf we invest" – **Herness Investment Management**

- "To improve the quality of human life by enabling people to do more, feel better and live longer" – **GlaxoSmithKline**

- "Improve people's lives through meaningful innovation" – **Philips**

- "Together we will make beauty sustainable. Together we will make sustainability beautiful" – **L'Oréal**.

- "Making sustainable living commonplace" – **Unilever**

- "Delivering experiences that our customers love for life – **Jaguar Land Rover**

- "To provide transportation as reliable as running water, everywhere for everyone." - **Uber**

- "To change the way the world travels and how people connect in the world" - **Airbnb**

- "To organise the world's information and make it universally accessible and useful" - **Google**.

You will now write your purpose statement. Here is my suggested process.

1. *Write your passion and purpose*

   ....

2. *Create your world reference poin*

   ....

3. *Define the values of the busines*

   ....

It is important that you write your company's mission statement, because it reflects your vision and enables your employees to commit to your vision.

Define a 'PURPOSE' for your organisation

Purpose

Definitions for business purpose are various, but we would argue a purpose is "the reason for operating its positive relevance to the world and its ability to inspire people." It is essential to state this and to understand it, because sometimes people confuse this with the means of doing something.

Purpose is WHY a business exists; it is what we aim to achieve in the world and for people rather than how we aim to achieve it.

When an organisation is powered by purpose, what a

business stands for becomes more important than what it sells.

- **Brompton Bicycles**'s stated purpose is "changing the way people live in cities"

- **Uber**'s is "to provide transportation as reliable as running water, everywhere for everyone."

- **Airbnb** is "changing the way the world travels and how people connect in the world."

Your vision: is significant because becoming purposeful requires a sense of what you are aspiring towards, your desire for a legacy in the change that purpose can bring and a conviction about where you want your organisation to be position.

If you don't ensure that your people are engaged, involved, and committed in the purpose of your business, how can you expect people to give their life's work, energy, time, and commitment to it?

Chuck Runyon and his business partner founded **Anytime Fitness** (www.anytimefitness.com) in 2002, and since then the franchise has grown to over 3000 locations in over 30 countries. Anytime Fitness is one of the largest and fastest-growing franchises in history, and Chuck shares the secret to their success: it's all about the people.

THE HOW

- Why inspires — We can all learn to lead if we start from our Why. Steve Ballmer, the CEO of Microsoft, was always highly enthusiastic and motivated through his emotional high tempo presentations. However, he was less able to inspire his people than the quietly spoken Bill Gates. Energy motivates, but charisma inspires. All great leaders have a greater depth of personality that is part of their authenticity — it's the clarity of their Why that inspires — an underlying belief and absolute conviction to a cause greater than who they are.

- <u>Leaders inspire and lead through the Why</u> — The leader's job is to encourage the organisation with the Why. If the CEO is the chief storyteller of the Why, then the senior management oversees the How. Underneath that is where the What is created. It is the What that brings the Why to life. The Vision of a company is the Why. The mission (i.e., task) is the strategy to get there — i.e., the How. A company needs both (that is why the book is called START with Why…).

- <u>Every Why person needs a How person to make the Why happen</u> — Often it takes over one person to make things happen. In Martin Luther King's case, it was Ralph Abernathy that knew the How (e.g., "Don't ride the buses"). Roy Disney was a How to type while Walt was a Why type. It was Roy who founded Buena Vista Distribution Company and created the merchandising arm. Paul Allen was Bill Gates' Why man. Rollin King was Herb Kelleher's Why man, and Steve Wozniak was Steve Job's Why man. Why types are visionaries and optimists. How types are more practical and live in the now. Why types can end up as starving visionaries without the aid of a How type. The Whys may have a vision, but it's the How's who turn it into a reality. Most successful entrepreneurs are How types as they make things happen.

- <u>Why drives authenticity and trust</u> — The Why is the critical part of building any relationship. Being authentic is increasingly essential in a transparent world. It's about consistency — where we do what we say and say what we do. Often, it's encapsulated in the statement of our values and beliefs (i.e., our Why). When we know a person is acting from a more profound sense of beliefs, then we are more likely to trust them. Their Why gives us an insight into the person — what is their driving motivation. When they do not reveal this, then we mistrust them (often applying more selfish reasons for their behaviour).

Credit: Sinek, Simon (2011) Start With Why: How Great Leaders Inspire Everyone To Take Action

Articulating Vision and Strategic Direction through Effective Communication

"Good business leaders create a vision, articulate the vision, passionately own the vision, and relentlessly drive it to completion." (Jack Welch, former CEO, GE).

Ability to articulate and communicate a vision, compelling strategic direction, and values clearly to all stakeholders across various mediums in a must for a leader in today's world.

According to the Oxford dictionary, vision is the ability to think about or plan the future with imagination or wisdom. Vision is a perpetual force. It is a critical anchor that drives decisions, actions and judgments.

Being a visionary mean that you must imagine the future sometimes with no reference points. Think of great names or even what you are sitting on now was once someone's vision and imagination

A CIPD report titled *'The Future of Talent in Singapore 2030'* documented said that *"leaders must communicate ideas to people of different cultural and educational backgrounds: to "reach people" from a diversity of backgrounds."*

When working with a global workforce, leaders will need the ability to communicate effectively across cultures. Like a location pointer on a GPS map, leaders must clarify the current situation concerning changing external demands continually. Equally crucial for leaders is to reiterate and reinforce vision, values and strategies. Finally, leaders must help others in clarifying the meaning of their work, communication and clarity being the currencies of effective leadership.

(Credit: Wong, W., Martorana, S. and Dunleavy, S., 2016. *The future of talent in Singapore 2030.* CIPD).

With a younger workforce that is purpose-driven, having a compelling vision for the future is also a key driver for engaging and keeping high-performing team members. A compelling vision is an essential pre-requisite for any community or network to succeed. Leaders who will thrive in a VUCA future are the ones who have a clear vision of where they want their organisations and teams to be.

Clint Burdett Strategic Consulting offers further insight into the need for language and directional precision by using the John F Kennedy's speech illustration.

"Perhaps the best example I know for clear and concise language asking for a core, fundamental commitment was:

"I believe that this nation should commit itself to achieving the goal, before this decade is out, of landing a man on the moon and returning him safely to the earth."

JFK, Man on the Moon Speech, Joint Session of Congress May 25, 1961

All seven critical components for a vision are there: __who__ (the nation), __what__ (land on the moon), __how__ (land a man on the moon), __the promise__ (return him safely), __geographic focus__ (The USA, but the message was to the world), __the goal__ (land a man on the moon and return him safely), and __when__ (by the end of the decade.)

It combines a purpose, mission, and vision with Presidential courtesy extended to the Congress."

(http://www.clintburdett.com/process/11_documents/documents_01_3_jfk_visi on.htm#.Wk-JBrdl_IU)

No question about it. Great leaders are great communicators. Even demagogues like Adolf Hitler swayed their followers, because they were able to communicate. This is not about filibuster tactics. Great communicators have a message and relay it well.

In his book, *Leading Change,* John P Kotter, said, "*Great visions are nothing if they cannot be communicated. Thus, use of story/metaphor, multiple media (people), simplicity and repetition, and leading by example all apply.*"

The most accurate test of your leadership potential is your ability to animate your audience with a passion for your cause. Can you remember the vision of Martin Luther King made famous in his 1963, "*I Have a Dream*" speech or Obama's "*Yes We Can*"? Or the vision of the biblical Moses taking the Israelites to the "land flowing with milk and honey"?

The key is your ability to tap into your listeners' best instincts. If you can remember that your speech is not all about you and your dedication to your mission, but about making your audience feel better about themselves, then you have a much better chance of generating excitement. We remember Mark Anthony, because of his oration at the funeral of Caesar in Shakespeare's popular play, *Julius Caesar.* Abraham Lincoln is famous among America's Presidents because of his famous Gettysburg address among others.

This is a template that you can use as a leader—7 Steps to making a great presentation

Making a presentation puts you on public display. An audience not only listens to your ideas, but it also responds to the way you use your voice and your body. You need more than a well-written presentation to make an impact. You will also need to deliver it in a lively, flexible and exciting way. This is a short framework on how to design and deliver a compelling presentation in style.

To begin with, imagine that you are in the audience for your presentation. What are those things that might:

- *Grab your attention?*

- *Stimulate your imagination?*

- *Inspire your confidence?*

- *Develop your understanding?*

Now think about ways to encourage these things.

1. DEFINE YOUR OBJECTIVE(S)

The starting point, the first question to ask is what is the purpose of the presentation; what are your objectives?

- What do you want them to do or change?

- What is your key message? Typically, a statement that says what you want them to do and why they will want to do it?

- What effect do you want to have?

- What result do you wish to achieve?

- What do you want your audience to think after your presentation?

- What do you want your audience to feel after your presentation?

- What do you want your audience to do after your presentation? Your message (a one-sentence, audience-focused message, written as if you are speaking to an individual)

- What problem does your talk address, and why is it so important to solve this problem?

Questions every audience asks...

- Am I going to benefit from what he/she talks about?

- Will he/she say anything valuable that I can take and use?

- Will anything that he/she says be worthwhile for me to act on?

  Build your presentation around the purpose of your speech, and what you want the audience to do differently.

2. DO YOUR AUDIENCE ANALYSIS

- Analysis—who are the audience members? How many will be there?

- Understanding—What is their knowledge level of the subject

- Demographic—What is their age, sex and educational background?

- Interest—Why will they be there, who ask them to come?

- Environment—Where will I stand? Will everyone in the audience be able to see me?

- Needs—What are the audience/listener's needs? What are your needs?

- Customised—How can I customise my message for this audience, by using specific techniques and anecdotes and by emphasising a particular aspect of my subject?

- Expectations—What do listeners expect to learn from me? What do I want the audience to do after my presentation?

3. TITLE YOUR SPEECH

- Give your speech an attention-grabbing title? Like **"How to Live Long in the 21st Century"**

4. HAVE AN INTRODUCTION/BEGINNING

Attention-grabbing opening

- A startling question
- A challenging statement
- An appropriate quotation
- An appropriate story or illustration
- A display of some appropriate object or picture
- Attention-getting generalisation

5. HAVE A BODY/MIDDLE

Clear structure

- Transition (signals moving from introduction to body)
- Main idea 1 (supporting ideas, details/examples, visual aids or props)
- Transition/signpost
- Main idea 2 (supporting ideas, details/examples, visual aids of props)
- Transition/signpost
- Main idea 3 (supporting ideas, details/examples, visual aids of props)
- Transition/signpost

6. OUTLINE RECAPS/SUMMARIES – KEY POINTS

7. HAVE A CONCLUSION/ENDING

Conclusive ending

- Memorable

- Inspiring

- Reinforce ideas

- Leave the audience with a lasting impression

- End forcefully and confidently

- Able to recommend a course of action

My 10 Tips for Speaking in Public

1. *Be yourself*: As a speaker, it is you they want to hear from - your views, your stories, what you think should be done, your interpretation of the facts.

2. *Structure your talk*: Your audience needs an outline or framework to help them follow what you are telling them. Make sure it has a clear beginning, middle, and end:

- Opening—you need a strong start to attract audience attention. Issue a challenge, state an issue, give a quote, ask a question.

- Body- have only three key points to your talk

- Conclusion—finish confidently and with conviction - a call to action, a challenge or a question.

3. *Eye contact*: always maintain eye contact with your audience - even when you are thinking about what to say next.

4. ***Speak from the heart and with passion and compassion for your audience***: Real conviction breeds enthusiasm. If you are listless and half-hearted, they will be too. Try not to read your speech — your commitment is your greatest asset. They need to see, hear and feel what it is you are telling them.

5. ***Keep it simple***: Tailor your speech to your audience. It is about what they need/want to know and not about how much you can tell them.

6. ***Remember the power of the pause***: in speechmaking, the power of silence can significantly add to the impact of your talk. Try it!

7. ***Use your voice and your body:*** gestures and vocal variety (pitch, pace, pause and volume) enhance your performance.

8. ***Speak to time***: don't go on for too long: give your talk/make your point(s) — and then sit down.

9. ***Practice. Practice. Practice***: Try it out in front of a mirror at home — it helps. Get feedback from your friends/boss or family members.

10. ***Speak Up! And Speak Out!*** Project your voice to the back of the room. Your voice needs to be heard — never say no to a speaking opportunity.

And above all... smile and enjoy it!

Nelson Mandela's closing remarks from his famous three-hour speech as defendant on 20 April 1964 is another brilliant instance.

"I have fought against white domination, and I have fought against black domination. I have cherished the ideal of a democratic and free society in which all persons live together in harmony and with equal opportunities. It is an ideal which I hope to live for and to achieve. But if needs be, it is an ideal for which I am prepared to die."

(Mandela, N., 1964. I Am Prepared to Die: Excerpts from Complete Text of the famous Speech in his defence at the Rivonia Trial. Christian Action. Source: Wikipedia)

1. BE AN EFFECTIVE COMMUNICATOR

Let us revisit a once-cited example. Mohammed bin Rashid Al Maktoum is the Prime Minister and Vice President of the United Arab Emirates (UAE), and absolute monarch of Dubai. A visionary leader renowned for the astounding and accentuated development of the region, Al Maktoum is credited with the following iconic sayings.

"All leaders dream. But only a true leader can turn a dream into a vision and a reality. Vision is the way to rule development and is also a matter of courage and conquering the impossible. It is believing in our ability to achieve our goals; a matter of having clear objectives and realising them with determination, efficiency and speed, never pausing until our children see their country competing with the world's most successful economic centres."

". .. I want to tap the potential of people, inspire them to generate ideas, help them develop wealth, and transform their ideas into major projects and job opportunities. Nothing is more important than people."

"Good leadership puts the interests of the community before those of any specific group. We can only establish the credibility of leadership through action and not words."

— Mohammed bin Rashid Al Maktoum (*My Vision Challenges in The Race for Excellence*)

"A true leader is one who creates a favourable environment to bring out the energy and ability of his team. A great leader creates more great leaders and does not reduce the institution to a single person." — Mohammed Bin Rashid Al Maktoum (*Flashes of Thought*)

"With each new day in Africa, a gazelle wakes up knowing he must

outrun the fastest lion or perish. At the same time, a lion stirs and stretches, knowing he must outrun the fastest gazelle or starve. It is no different for humanity. Whether you consider yourself a gazelle or a lion, you simply have to run faster than others to survive." - Mohammed bin Rashid Al Maktoum (*My Vision: Challenges in the Race for Excellence*)

2. LEADING FROM THE FRONT

"That way, I never ask people to do something that I haven't done. It gives you credibility and makes everything authentic. My first level of people to inspire are the next level of leaders following me, the independent sales directors, they, in turn, inspire the consultants in their units. So, everything trickles down to our foundation" — Chief (Mrs) E. Ozua, NSD, Mary Kay UK.

When Gordon Bethune took over Continental in 1994, he knew *"it was a crummy place to work"*. He saw his first responsibility to look after his employees and build their trust and belief that they could turn the place around. He wanted it to be a family pulling together.

Bethune said, *"You can't lie to your Doctor, and you can't lie to your employees"*. Happy employees lead to happy customers, and happy customers lead to happy shareholders — in that order.

One of the key things he did was change the metrics as this shifts the behavioural focus of an organisation (for example, to be focused on planes running on time and away from just financial targets).

He also concreted his words in actions. For example, he instituted an open-door policy and took away security on the 20th floor. He would help load bags, and he gave out a flat bonus to everyone of $65 every-time they hit their target (sent out as a separate cheque with a note attached saying "Thank you for helping make Continental one of the best").

In 1994 the airline lost $600m. The next year Continental posted profits of $250m and was soon ranked as one of the best companies to work for.

3. SET CLEAR GOALS AND PRIORITY

You can't inspire action unless you first clarify expectations and priorities.

Define results within the organisation and each department. Without clarity around outcomes, no one can be accountable.

Practice **"carefrontation"** — the careful and caring confrontation of others.

When you challenge people, you inspire them to stay focused.

Set stretch goals — they energise people.

Golden Thread

Everyone must know why/what they are working for and how the job punches the company forward. The Golden thread. Give people a sense of responsibility and make them feel that their actions make a difference.

4. INVEST IN THEM

Improving and advancing the skills and professionalism of every person in your company is an ongoing process, and formal training sessions should be regular and non-negotiable.

Coach them

You must train and coach your people to enhance their learning ability and performance. Coaching is the key to unlocking the potential of your people, your organisation, and yourself. It increases your effectiveness as a leader. As a coach, you must help your people grow and achieve more by inspiring them, asking practical questions and providing feedback. Find the right combination of instructor-led training and coaching follow-ups to achieve success.

Give people the right tools

"If you give people the right tools, and make them more productive, then everyone, no matter their lot in life, will have an opportunity to achieve their real potential." - Sinek (2009)

5. THE CLIMATE OF TEAMWORK

Climate

Amy Edmondson (Novartis Professor of Leadership and Management - Harvard Business School) reinforces this thinking in her concept of 'Psychological Safety' and explains why this is critical to 'Teaming'. The term psychological safety describes a climate in which people express relevant thoughts and feelings. This is critical to allow people to be authentic, reveal vulnerabilities and gain trust for the creation of inspirational climates that will enable teams to flourish.

In *'Teaming: How organisations learn, innovate and compete in the knowledge economy'*, Amy explains: *"Teaming, coined deliberately to capture the activity of working together, presents a new, more flexible way for organisations to carry out interdependent tasks. Unlike the traditional concept of a team, teaming is an active process, not a static identity. Imagine a fluid network of interconnected individuals working in temporary teams (in a psychologically safe environment) on improvement, problem-solving and innovation. Teaming blends relating to people, listening to other points of view, coordinating action and making shared decisions... Teaming calls for the development of affective (feeling) and cognitive (thinking) skills."* (Amy Edmondson, 2012)

Ask what effective communication is?

When the right information gets to the right person at the right time.

- **Trust**

  Do they know that they can trust that you have their back in all situations? How well do you know their worries, future goals etc. (individualised consideration)

- **Camaraderie**

  Are you visible (an invisible barrier that they may not cross) in an open-plan office or more remote (when people don't feel that they know you, they keep their distance)? Both have advantages and disadvantages.

  Suggest doing a walk and talk when addressing tricky scenarios (neutralises the power complex)

- **Safety**

  Communication is rock solid when people feel secure and confident. Applaud strengths and work with your team's weaknesses. Instead of saying why did you do that, start with… help me understand your thinking around this…?

- **Clarity**

  Breakdowns occur when you're vague. Depending upon the situation, sometimes you must reinforce the message in a variety of ways - verbally, written, video. And sometimes you must say it in a slightly different way.

- **Teamwork**

   Teamwork is essential for competing in today's global arena. Build a star team, not a team of stars. Diversity of thought, perception, background and experience enhance creativity and innovation.

   In today's complex world, an agile organisation will adapt, grow, and progress. Belgian author, Frederic Laloux, identifies these agile organisations as 'Teal Organisations' — evolutionary and purpose-driven. His book, *'Reinventing Organisations'* is considered by many to be the most influential management book of this decade and is widely accepted as most inspiring to a whole range of organisations by prompting them to adopt a whole different outlook and practice on key management principles.

   "The 'Teal' environment is open, honest, encourages risk-taking, tolerates failure and learns fast. This climate enables inspiration and innovation to flow and grow. This environment is enhanced by a diverse workforce, where ideas are openly shared, diversity is respected, and people work in teams." Mutual respect exists, and we value individuals and teams; people are aligned to the purpose of the organisation. Inspirational Leadership is the catalyst to make this happen.

- **The cadence of shared accountability**

Institute a cadence of shared accountability. When accountability only exists between each team member and their boss, its effect is limited, but when team members feel accountable to each other, their performance shifts from being professional to personally extraordinary. Our experience has consistently shown that people will work hard to avoid disappointing their boss, but they will work harder to avoid disappointing their team. The result is a dramatically increased level of performance and follow-through.

(Source: *The 4 Disciplines of Execution: Achieving Your Wildly Important Goals* by Chris McChesney, Jim Huling, and Sean Covey).

- **Promote inclusion**

To experience success, people also need to feel included. Inclusion and integration go beyond the realm of listening and providing feedback. For real inclusion, people need to feel intimately connected to the actions and process that are leading to the accomplishment of the goals or the final decision.

6. CREATE A CULTURE OF INNOVATION AND EXECUTION

In a 2011 article for the *MIT Sloan Management Review*, Julian Birkinshaw and colleagues concluded that *'Innovation is the lifeblood of any large organisation.'*

Take the innovative outlook of these frontline organisations, for example.

- **Audi**: "create the best brand experience through innovative and emotional products."

- **Samsung Electronics**: "dedicated to developing innovative technologies and efficient processes that create new markets, enrich people's lives and continue to make Samsung a digital leader."

Innovation should be anchored in the company's ambition, so it has both contexts and is a sustainable part of the corporate fabric. Talking about change is easy, but you must support what you say with what you can see in the organisation — the structures and systems that support and reward innovation are balanced with creativity and autonomy—and this translates into what you do and how you do things. Let's now look at the finer details of the two innovative brands cited earlier.

AUDI

Today, under the leadership of Ferdinand Piëch, the Volkswagen Group is aiming to become the largest, most profitable business in its market. It was widely expected to have overtaken Toyota as the global #1 manufacturer by 2018.

Audi's global production had grown from 354,000 in 1993 to 1.09 million in 2010: sales have just overtaken Mercedes and are forecast to surpass BMW by 2014. Audi aims to become the number one premium brand in its sector by using its expertise, passion, and agility to *'create the best brand experience through innovative and emotional products'* that all bring to life its core brand values of being 'sophisticated, progressive and sporty.'

The role of design key to Audi's strategy to become the number 1 brand is its focus on leading-edge design, both in terms of technical engineered design and aesthetic product design. And this is not a new approach. *"Audi design is distinctive—it is the harmony of form and function,"* says Royal College of Art trained Stefan Sielaff, head of design at Audi AG. *"Above all, it is the proportions, the sculptures of our automobiles which portray the interplay of technology and design. This philosophy has a remarkable past—it is the key facet in Audi's history."* Audi is now recognised across the industry as the design benchmark—not only for external form but also for interiors where, from a quality and craftsmanship point of view, the company is up with the very best of the high-end brands like Aston Martin and Bentley.

Technology Landmarks: Audi's use of technology to lead brand development can be traced to 1971, when the company, with a growing range of respected models, started using the *'Vorsprung Durch Technik'* slogan to share the intent behind them. Translating as *'Progress through technology,'* this line has been used in advertising campaigns across the world and remains central to the brand's ethos and communications.

It cemented this approach in 1974 when Dr. Ferdinand Piëch, grandson of Ferdinand Porsche, became Audi's head of technical development. He not only rose to run the brand, and subsequently the entire Volkswagen Group, but crucially for Audi, he oversaw the development of several award-winning technological innovations including the five-cylinder engine, introducing four-wheel drive, and aluminium body shells, and the adoption of aerodynamic design.

The fundamental philosophy of its design-led approach enables Audi to make different choices from its competitors. If Mercedes is driven by comfort and BMW by improving performance to create the ultimate driving experience, Audi starts with the design and is good at it. Over five years, Audi has won the world's 'best performance car' award three times: in 2007 with the RS4; in 2008 for the R8 sports car; and again in 2010, with the V10 version of the R8. In recent years, Audi has won more design awards than any other brand, with two models seen as being game-changers in the sector.

SAMSUNG

Samsung Electronics is the world's largest consumer electronics company. Producing everything from phones, TVs, cameras, and laptops to microwaves and freezers, it is a top-three brand in pretty much every category in which it is active. The sales in 2010 were more than $135 billion, with net profits of over $14 billion. Samsung Electronics is now twice the size of Sony, the company which 20 years ago was the undisputed leader in the sector. While

Sony's revenues grew by 22% total in the last decade, Samsung Electronics' revenue rose by over 400% and, over the past five years, the company has maintained growth at an average of 16% every year.

In the TV market, Samsung Electronics has been a market leader by a good margin over Sony and local rival LG since 2006 and is way ahead in LCD panels; in the camera market it is number 2 to Sony and despite intense competition; in the cell phone market, Samsung Electronics has just over 20% of the global market and is rapidly closing in on Nokia.

Most significantly, in the DRAM and NAND flash memory arenas, where it competes with Intel and Toshiba, Samsung has over 40% of the market share. This is hugely important because it highlights how, even when not used in Samsung-branded products, its technologies are often found in those of its competitors: Samsung Electronics wins both ways.

The company is part of the larger $200 billion revenue Samsung Group that accounts for a fifth of Korea's exports.

Samsung has become the flagship of the South Korean economy and the source of much of the innovation that is taking place across the consumer electronics sector. Given that it was a low-cost 'me-too' manufacturer of imitations of Sharp's microwaves in the 1970s, this is a considerable achievement.

Whereas people used to look at Philips, Sony, and Toshiba for the latest developments, today it is Apple and Samsung Electronics. As Apple has moved across some consumer electronics markets with its high margin products, it has become the only real challenger to Samsung's dominance. Pivotal to Samsung Electronics' success over the past decade has been the way it has embraced design as the source of competition.

From 2 to 900, the Samsung Electronics design team now consistently takes most awards at the prestigious annual design events as the company's products are time and time again seen as leading the category in performance, quality, and value.

The Early Years

Born out of the larger Samsung chaebol which was in the food-processing and textiles sectors, Samsung Electronics started in 1969, manufacturing low-cost black and white TVs, fridges, microwaves, and washing machines.

Although by the early 1990s Samsung Electronics had grown to be a significant manufacturer with its products sold around the world, at heart this firm was still producing low-end products and, in its part of the market, was facing increasing competition. To grow, it needed to continue to win in its core area but also move upmarket and compete at a higher level.

Top of Form

To become more innovative, Samsung Electronics needed a cultural transformation, and a vital part of this was in creating a facility for nurturing and developing talent. 'In 1995, the company set up the Innovative Design Lab of Samsung (IDS), an in-house school where promising designers could study under experts from the Art Centre College of Design in Pasadena, California, one of the top US design schools. Samsung designers were dispatched to Egypt and India, Paris and Frankfurt, New York and Washington to tour museums, visit icons of modern architecture, and explore ruins.'

Although Samsung Electronics was a technology-and process-obsessed company, this laid the seeds for how it would become more competitive by placing design centre-stage.

To quote Laurie J Mullins in the book, *Management and Organisational Behaviour*, "According to a recent CBI report: 'Effective *leaders, who can inspire their people to realise their personal and collective potential are often the deciding factors between a company being good at what it does and achieving greatness'.*" (p363)

Tony Elumelu

Elumelu is the Chairman of the UBA Group. He shares these thoughts-

- Execution: A burning desire to always see things through to completion in a timely, efficient and effective manner. We believe in hard work and seeing through ideas from conception throughout to achieving excellent results.

- The inspirational leader listens to the people in her organisation. Talking to people about your passion is not enough. To share meaning—a favourite and meaningful definition of communication—you must allow the ideas and thoughts of your staff to help form the vision and mission, or minimally, the goals and action plan. No one is ever one hundred percent supportive of a direction they had no part in formulating.

7. GIVE CONSTRUCTIVE FEEDBACK

The Sandwich Technique to Deliver Bad News or Complaints

Among the many etiquette skills presented in our seminars, the one I enjoy sharing most is one of the simplest. It's the Sandwich Technique; the tool managers use when they must deliver unpleasant news, resolve conflict, address a troubling situation, or make a constructive complaint.

It's easy and effective. Compliments and positive statements "sandwich" each side of the unpleasant news, thus making it easier to digest.

Follow these tips for best results:

i. Begin the conversation with a genuine compliment and positive statement about the person in a non-judgmental, calm, and friendly tone of voice.

ii. When moving into the meat of the matter, use transition words such as regrettably, unfortunately, or however. Be specific. It's best to state only two items to improve. This is not the time to air your laundry list of gripes.

iii. Remain calm throughout and speak in a low and even tone of voice. State the facts and don't get emotional.

iv. Maintain an open and inviting body language. You don't want to appear closed off, with your arms or hands folded.

v. When an apology is warranted, don't skirt it. Say "I'm sorry" or "I apologise" and show sincere regret. (Check this portal for further reading:

http://www.advancedetiquette.com/2012/09/saying-im-sorry-and-meaning-it/)

vi. Suggest specific ways to resolve the matter so the two of you can move forward.

vii. End with positive and encouraging statements that will help renew the relationship and allow everyone involved to feel good about the conversation that just took place.

viii. Follow up a few days later to see how the person felt about the conversation and confirm all is resolved or if further discussion is needed.

Its application is infinite. Use the Sandwich Technique to:

• Give feedback to employees, supervisors, and co-workers

- Resolve personal situations with family members, relatives, friends, and neighbours

- Express your complaints to vendors, suppliers, store personnel and the public

If you practise this technique and make it a part of your life, you will be on the path to good leadership. You will be someone who cares about maintaining a relationship whenever an adverse situation arises. We all have conflicts in our lives. What's important is how we handle them. The Sandwich Technique lets you build and maintain relationships without tearing down friendships or professional relationships. I hope you try it soon.

(http://www.advancedetiquette.com/2012/10/the-sandwich-technique-to-deliver-bad-news-or-complaints/)

Balanced performance appraisal

A general ratio to consider is 3:1. That means for every development area; you should consider three positive areas of performance. Would you need to reconsider this ratio if you are planning on managing the individual's performance as a capability issue?

Though the context of feedback will drive it:

- the staff member's previous performance

- the staff member's current performance

- the expectations of the role now

- the expectations of the position

Evidenced clear and measurable data of an individual's performance that is easily comparable to their objectives. Think about the target set we covered earlier:

Good performance objectives will have clear success criteria, i.e., clear measures to state how well they have been completed.

Sensitive — You have a responsibility as a manager to respond to the needs of the person receiving the feedback. This is important if you must discuss areas of poor performance.

Beforehand, it's useful to ask yourself how your employee prefers to receive feedback. Some people respond well to direct criticism; most, however, need encouragement to identify areas of under-achievement.

Take some time beforehand to think about how you will approach the area of concern. We will look at difficult conversations in more details later in this section.

Timely - The context of the activity, and the level of under-achievement, will drive the most appropriate time to give feedback on a capability issue. Occasionally, it is essential to provide feedback to someone immediately, for example, if the actions of the employee put their or another's safety at risk.

In most circumstances, the feedback can be delivered later. Take care though not to store up a long list of negative areas of performance to be delivered in a 1-1 supervision; if you are concerned over an individual's performance, make them aware and speak with them as soon as is practical.

Ask them; what were the distinct differences between the two models, BEST and ABCDE?

What situations do you think each is appropriate?

ABCDE — less severe? Positive feedback?

BEST — More serious?

8. INTEGRITY

If you promised the moon, deliver it along with a handful of stars. Delivering on your promises is doing what you say you will do when you say you will do it. Every time you follow through on a commitment, small or large, you build trust.

Also, leaders need to pay their staff salaries as at when due. This is part of integrity.

Integrity - A trusted brand that keeps to its promises

The integrity **of the person leading.** Yes, vision and passion are essential, but your employees must trust you if you want them to feel inspired. They must believe in your integrity and see it played out in decisions and customer and employee treatment.

They must believe in you. Your **person** is as important as the direction you provide. Employees look up to a person who tells the truth, tries to do the right things, lives a **good**, principled life, and who does their best. Trust this. Your actions play out on the stage of your organization. And your staff boos and cheer and vote with their feet and their activities. Your human behaviour that has congruity with your speaking and acting is always at the centre stage.

9. REMEMBER YOUR PEOPLE ARE YOUR BEST ASSET – TREAT THEM WELL

"Train people well enough so they can leave, treat them well enough so they don't want to." — Richard Branson, Founder of Virgin Group employing about 65,000 people across the world.

To create an environment where employees feel valued, recognise their achievements. While money is a motivator, so are praise, recognition, rewards and noticing an individual's contribution to a successful endeavour.

Speaking directly to a contributing employee about the value that their work provides for the organisation is a crucial source of inspiration for the recipient.

10. MAKE BUSINESS FUN

Make people want to come to work. As a business today is about passion and creating new things, the fun has become a significant element in the business strategy of many highly successful companies. Make fun of an essential part of your corporate culture to enable relentless innovation and create an inspiring corporate culture. People should be happy at work and have fun. Encourage just fun programmes. *"Find some humour in your failures. Don't take yourself too seriously. Loosen up, and everybody will loosen up. Have fun. Show enthusiasm – always"*.

(**https://www.slideshare.net/Dr.Rajesh/inspirational-leadership**)

Invest in your knowledge bank

- It may not follow that all readers are leaders, but all leaders are readers. Stay informed.

- Tell people about books that have inspired you. Share the knowledge.

- Others are; curiosity, observation, listening and travelling

- When you stay informed, you stay engaged with people, and you inspire them.

Great Leaders Inspire everyone to act

Leaders inspire – Successful leaders do not run companies – they lead movements. Great leaders do something exceptional – they inspire us to act. Leading means people want to follow (rather than have to follow).

Let me end this chapter with words of John Quincy Adams' (6th US President) *"If your actions inspire others to dream more, learn more, do more and become more, you are a leader."*

Show APPRECIATION

One of the greatest gifts a leader can give his followers is that of genuine appreciation. For most people, and most businesses, however, conducting their business life, and their various interpersonal human relationships with appreciation as a constant and premium currency on offer can be like trying to navigate uncharted waters. Any seasoned sailor will tell you that navigating previously uncharted waters can be a very daunting task. Therefore, we need a North Star in our task of empathic and ethical navigation.

In my sincere opinion, the Golden Rule can be our North Star in this quest.

In its most straightforward, and perhaps most lucid expression, the Golden Rule states: "*Do unto others as you would have others do unto you.*" Being the closest entity to a universal guideline for ethical conduct we can find, the Golden Rule seems to cut across a myriad of cultural settings and religious boundaries, and is embraced by people from nearly every part of the world. For instance, Islam declares: "*No one of you is a believer until he loves for his neighbour what he loves for himself.*" Judaism puts it this way: "*What is hateful to you, do not do (it) to your fellow man. This is the entire Law; all the rest is commentary.*" The Buddhist version is slightly shorter but no less succinct: "*Hurt not others with that which pains yourself.*" Hinduism says: "*This is the sum of duty; do not unto others what you would not have them do unto you.*"

Those who wish to communicate their desire to employ a decent and honest standard of ethical and appreciative conduct in relating to others, easily find sufficient motivation in the Golden Rule. Such confidence in the universal applicability of this relatively simple rule is, perhaps, understandable on individual bases:

One, most people find it easy to accept the Golden Rule. Even if we were to base the universal acceptance of the Golden Rule on common sense alone, we would still be on firm ground. We would have to stretch our imagination to its limits to conceive of someone saying, "Please treat me worse than I treat you!" On the contrary, everyone wants to be treated well. It merely is not unreasonable to desire good treatment from others. Even those who engage in self-destructive behaviour do not consciously seek to be maltreated by others. One of the most fundamental rules of human relations is to seek common ground with others. Comparing similar experiences and discovery of shared beliefs will usually pave the way for a successful relationship. The Golden Rule can create this familiar turf with any other person.

Two, the Golden Rule is easy to understand. With the Golden Rule, you don't need more than a rudimentary knowledge of the law. You need not be a philosopher. All that is required from you is to imagine yourself in the place of another person.

Three, it is a win-win philosophy. Many people believe that for them to be winners, other people must be made to lose. They seem to see everyone as an enemy that must be subdued, and they relish capitalising on the pain of others to win. When we elect to live by the Golden Rule, everybody wins, since, if I treat you as well as I desire to be treated, you win; and if you treat me as you desire to be treated, I win. So, where is the loser in this scenario? It is a win for everybody. It promises a victory for employers. It promises a win for clients, and it promises success for employees.

At their very core, all people are very much the same regarding how they want to be treated.

Primarily, people want to be valued and appreciated. It is a documented fact that fully eighty percent of people who voluntarily leave their jobs do so because they do not feel valued and recognised at the workplace. This statistic grossly indicts most employers as people who treat their employees rather poorly. Even in purely interpersonal and domestic settings, most people want others to accept them for who they are and demonstrate through their action that they matter. Encouragement is rightly said to be oxygen for the soul. Valuing other people, not for their performance, but because they are foremost, human beings are the bedrock of the Golden Rule.

Also, people want to be truly appreciated. We all primordially need to be appreciated for what we can do. It is also a fact that we want to be appreciated for the skill and effort we deploy to our work. The mere knowledge that what we do matters to others boosts our confidence and self-esteem. As a human relations expert, Donald Laird, puts it: "*Always help people increase their self-esteem. Develop your skill in making other people feel important. There is hardly a higher compliment you can pay an individual than helping him to be useful and to find satisfaction in his usefulness.*" You can achieve this by letting people know you appreciate their efforts. Thank people at any opportunity. It is also an invaluable confidence booster to praise people in the presence of others. As a rule of the thumb, it is of great value to imagine that anyone you relate with is carrying a banner across his chest that proclaims, "Make me feel important!"

Again, people want to be trusted. Trust is the foundation of all good relationships. Functional business interactions, good friendships and good marriages all require trust. Without trust, there can be no open and honest relationship. When there is a foundation of trust in an organisation, people tend not only to communicate openly, vision and values, but they also show respect for employees, focusing on shared goals rather than their agenda. Such people listen with an open mind and can maintain confidences while demonstrating uncommon compassion. Experience has shown that the only way a man can be made trustworthy is by trusting him. Investing confidence in others is not an easy task to pursue, and it takes a genuine leap of faith, especially when we do not know them very well. However, we always remember that we also desire for people to invest in us.

That is the ultimate utility of the Golden Rule.

On another note, people want to be respected. It is only when you genuinely appreciate someone that you can treat him with respect. Respect cloaks people with dignity, building their confidence. It is said in some quarters that a man who does not respect his own life and that of others robs himself of his dignity as a human being. Most people desire the respect of the people they work for, and when employers give it freely, it creates a very positive working environment. James Howell once said: "*Respect a man, and he will do the more.*" How true this is! The quality of respect employees receive gives them the impetus to perform not only at their best but also with the incentive to work with excellence. Everyone benefits: the employee is honoured, and it is good for business.

People also want to be understood. A lack of understanding precipitates one of the greatest of man's communication difficulties. Often, we find ourselves ever so hasty to find fault with others when they do not conform to our standards. But if we attempt to understand them, we often discover that their way is not the wrong way - it is merely a different way. They may respond differently because they haven't had the advantages we have.

They may react to conditions that are entirely beyond their control. Once we transcend these interpersonal constraints, we can gain an emotional connectedness with others, and this is what understanding is all about. When dealing with others, we must always seek first to understand and then to be understood. This is the Fifth habit in the highly acclaimed book by Stephen Covey, *The Seven Habits of Highly Effective People*. The ability to seek first to understand others before being understood demands an attitude of emotional malleability and inherent humility. Without doubt, to appreciate another person properly will involve learning from him, which comprises an alteration in one's attitude.

To understand another person requires stretching out oneself to meet the person on his level and placing the entire responsibility of establishing a human connection entirely on oneself and not on the other person. As the famous inventor, Charles Kettering, once said, *"There is a great difference between knowing and understanding: You can know a lot about something and not understand it."* The same truism holds for interpersonal human relationships. This is the real basis for the skilled and proficient practice of empathic communication.

Finally, people do not want others to take advantage of them. The story is famously told of a highly sought- after management consultant who was requested by a billionaire businessman to beat back one of his many companies into profitable shape professionally. After carefully examining the distressed company's problems, and after a careful analysis of the tycoon's unorthodox approach to business, the renowned consultant, despite the apparent high regard in which his prospective client held him, expressed the sincere regret that he could not take up the commission to turn the company around. He could engage in such forthrightness because values, to him, occupied a much higher premium than money did. It would have been infinitely easy for the consultant to take advantage of the hapless billionaire. He could have conveniently rationalised fleecing money from the tycoon and giving next to nothing of value back to him, for the man was worth billions and would not have missed it. That, however, is not the moral point here. It does not matter whether we are talking about lying to a friend or defrauding a blue-chip company. Any action will ultimately impact on people, for better or for worse. What should always be uppermost in our mind is that if that action, whatever it is, takes undue advantage of them, it will ultimately hurt them so we would not like to be hurt. The Golden Rule would have been ingloriously violated.

We all need constant reminders to treat others as we would

like to be treated. When a person has an accurate and noble sense of how he wants to be treated with respect, dignity, trust and understanding-then, he can easily articulate in his mind how he should treat others. This will take his communication skill to the rarefied pedestal of the empathic, which, truly, is the ultimate form of appreciation.

Business tycoon Richard Branson writing on his blogsite stated: "*People are what have made Virgin what it is today, and my philosophy has always been (to) treat staff how you would want to be treated. Train people well so they can leave, treat them well enough, so they don't want to. Rigid corporate culture doesn't inspire people to think creatively and come up with innovative solutions. You get a lot more done when you get rid of the formalities and hierarchies. I may have been knighted, but I always prefer it when people call me Richard – leaders should be approachable and everyone should be treated the same. If you call your cleaner by their first name, then you should also do the same for your CEO or founder.*"

Source: 'How to lead the next generation' by Richard Branson, 11 October 2017 https://virgin.co.uk/branson-family/richard-branson-blog/how-lead-next-generation accessed Monday 21 December 2020 21:12hrs)

In the July–August 2020 issue of *Harvard Business Review*, Stewart Butterfield, CEO of Slack said, "**What leaders must do above all else in times like these is remind people of what's important, emphasizing an organization's foundational tenets, its purpose and mission, and the impact it can have, and constantly expressing gratitude for the hard work they're doing to execute on those things**".

Now that many staff are working from home you may need to adapt your leadership style to keep staff motivated and inspire action.

Here are some practical ways to keep your virtual team motivated:

- Practice active listening; paraphrase what your employees say in order to confirm understanding, since there are more opportunities for misunderstandings without visual cues

- Don't assume that your instructions are clear; have team members summarize the assigned task before taking it on

- Make yourself available outside normal business hours

- Minimize the use of email; encourage team members to schedule conversations with each other as they collaborate on a project

- Instant messaging tools like Google Hangouts, Google Talk, Microsoft Lync (now Skype for Business) and Cisco Jabber allow you to check in with team members in a way that's less formal

- Make it easy for all employees to access the documents they need remotely. Using cloud-based file-sharing software, such as Google Drive or Dropbox, can help everyone easily share documents and stay organized

- Providing constructive feedback through virtual coaching sessions is another important way to keep team members motivated

Credit: https://iveybusinessjournal.com/how-to-lead-an-effective-virtual-team/

Summary – Chapter 7

1   Action-centered leadership is key to success.

2   Effective leadership requires communication skills.

3   Vision is not enough, you should enforce it

4   People are not only interested in the why but the how you do something

Chapter 8

Resilience - Overturning adversity (Attribute 6)

W ithin the pervading context of VUCA, the attendant turbulence already connotes the existence of challenges, which can only be, in the long run, adversity in one form or the other. The ability to surmount adversity, in whatever way, represents one's index of resilience in a VUCA world.

Ultimately, we will have to be grateful for our challenges. Whenever you encounter a significant challenge, you should, in real and practical terms, be thankful for it. Many people meet their inevitable difficulties with complaining and garnish it with feeling pathetically sorry for themselves. The salient truth, however, is that it is an ineffectual and unproductive attitude. Instead, attempt to realise that, in every adversity, is an equal or more significant benefit. It has been proven, repeatedly, that if you look hard enough, there is always a good side to every potentially harmful situation. Could you conceivably see an opportunity to learn and grow? This simple change in perception can transform a challenge into something positive, with long-term benefits. However, for that to happen, you will need to cultivate an attitude of gratitude.

Handling adversity, which is an inevitability in coping with the VUCA times, is asking you to be at your best when things are at their worst.

Professor Randy Pausch occupied a Carnegie Mellon-endowed professorial chair. When the amiable teacher discovered that he had terminal cancer, he decided that his final lecture would revolve around the most important lessons he'd learned in his life. When things were at their worst, he created something beautiful, and his clear and thoughtful delivery left his family and the rest of the world, a timeless treasure.

As he eloquently put it, *"We cannot change the cards we are dealt, just how we play the hand."*

The salient question now becomes, "how do great leaders play the bad cards they are dealt?"

The indisputable and very comforting thought is that the most impressively resilient leaders the world has known have been courageous in the face of great adversity, and the challenges of life lift them instead of knocking them down.

On 3rd of April 2009 - to be precise - I was at the Holiday Inn, Accra, Ghana for a speaking engagement. After the gig, I updated my journal and wrote that in the next five years, I would like to share the stage with my one of my speaking mentors, Les Brown. After Ghana, I went to Lagos for a speaking engagement before coming back to the UK. When I got back to the UK, I received a message from the promoter of an event, Herald Bradnock that he'll like me to speak at Central Hall, Westminster alongside Les

Brown. I was like, oh my God! This is the Lord's doing; it is marvellous in my eyes. I prepared very well. I was the only British speaker who was invited to speak alongside those from America. They said I would speak before Les on 2 September 2009 in front of 2000 people, at Central Hall Westminster in Central London. That was the place where President Obama spoke when he came to England. Dr Nelson Mandela has spoken there. That's one of the most celebrated landmark venues/buildings in the United Kingdom.

The previous week was very good. It was my busiest in my speaking career, about six engagements. I also won two awards as the Best Emcee in the UK and the Best Motivational Speaker of the Year.

But the Monday of that speaking engagement, 31st August 2009, my mother died! I was preparing for this big gig when they called me that my mother had died. It shattered me. My mum died on Monday. On Wednesday, I had my most significant speaking engagement. Should I cancel, should I go ahead? And you know the unfortunate thing was that if I cancelled, they would not miss me! Because I wasn't the main speaker — Les Brown, the world's leading motivational speaker, was headlining. I would have missed the greatest opportunity of my life by not speaking at that place. But something now occurred to me. I asked myself what would happen if I were to be the lead speaker, and they paid me £10,000? Was I going to return the £10,000? What will my mother want me to do? I know that she will want me to do the gig. Hence, I decided to do the gig.

On my way to the venue, I stopped by at Westminster Abbey to pray. I remember that I prayed for the spirit of boldness, and I meditated on Stephen's speech to the Sanhedrin in Acts of Apostle, Chapter 7. On the night, I was to speak for about seven minutes on the power of self-belief using my story. In my concluding remarks, I told the audience that my mother died two days ago and she's still in the mortuary. Les Brown led the standing ovation, and people were moved to tears. I was in tears of joy myself. He said something to me that night that I will never forget, "*Dayo, seek help not because you are weak, but because you want to be strong.*"

After my mother's funeral, I went for counselling, which I found very helpful to help me cope with my mother's death.

One thing I have learnt is that adversity strengthens us. Like in baking bread, the greater the heat, the bigger and better the bread becomes. Adversities allow successful people to develop new strengths and etch their statements on life with deep conviction.

Napoleon Hill, author and writer, asserted in his best-selling book 'Think and Grow Rich' that "*every adversity brings with it the seed of an equivalent advantage.*" What the author is invariably saying is that there is an advantage in every adversity that comes our way. There is a stepping-stone in every stumbling block we experience. There is a gain in every pain we go through.

After a series of failures, disappointments and unfavourable situations, Ralph Waldo Emerson concluded that "*our greatest glory is not in failing, but in rising every time we fail.*" 'Failing' in this context is a stumbling block, but if we sit on the fact that we fell and refuse to rise again, it then remains a stumbling block. Conversely, if we can change our approach and reactions to such failures, it automatically becomes a stepping-stone.

When setbacks or tragedies occur, never, ever give up; instead see them as opportunities for growth because success thrives on adversity.

Great champions are known to snatch victory from the jaws of defeat. I have read stories of many men who bounced back after being hit by adversity. Lee Iacocca turned the fortunes of Chrysler around when nobody gave him a chance

ACCEPTANCE is the first key in overcoming adversity

Leaders must accept that they do not have solutions to all problems and we now live in a VUCA world and this is the era of the Fourth Industrial Revolution. A leader must do something about it. A leader must also accept when things go wrong.

The wisdom of acceptance nests comfortably in an attitude of accepting and cooperating with the inevitable. This apt quote from a friend of mine says it all:

"I seek the fortitude to accept that which I can do nothing about.

I seek the strength to act on that which I can do something about.

I seek the wisdom to know the difference between the two."

Let us take an all-too-human story as an immediate illustration of the valuable power inherent in a courageous decision to cooperate with the inevitable. Newton Booth Tarkington was an American novelist and dramatist best known for his novels '*The Magnificent Ambersons,*' and '*Alice Adams.*' He is, with William Faulkner and John Updike, one of only three novelists to win the Pulitzer Prize for Fiction more than once. There was a statement that was credited to him: "*I could take anything that life could force upon me except one thing: blindness. I could never endure that.*"

Life was to deal him later a hand that was a paradoxical quirk of fate. One day, when he was in his sixties, Tarkington glanced down at the carpet in his study. The colours were blurred, and he could not visualise the pattern. An eye specialist told him the tragic truth. He was losing his eyesight. One eye was already almost entirely blind, while the other was expected to follow suit.

What Tarkington feared most had come upon him. Ordinarily, given his past pronouncements on how he might view such a harrowing possibility, he might have been expected to see the situation as the end of his life. But, to his amazement, and that of those close to him, he adopted a rather gay attitude to what might have seemed a hopeless situation. His attitude was the classic definition of the term "indomitable spirit."

Fate can never conquer such a spirit.

Finally, when he went blind, and the darkness closed in around him, this is what he told the world: "*I found I could take the loss of my eyesight, just as a man can take anything else. If I lost all five of my senses, I know I could live on inside my mind. For, it is in the mind that we see, and in mind, we live, whether or not we know it.*"

Tarkington would later go through a harrowing experience because, hoping to restore his eyesight, he had to endure over twelve operations within a year. Those were in the days when the only available form of anaesthesia was local. He did not rail against it. He knew it had to be done, and since there was no escaping the ordeal, the only option left was to take his suffering with stoic grace. He declined to stay in a private room and instead preferred to stay in an open ward where he could be with other patients with troubles of their own. He attempted to cheer them up. Even when he had to submit to repeated surgeries, fully conscious of the traumatic invasion of his eyes, he fell back on how fortunate he was. He would say, "*How wonderful! How wonderful that science now has the skill to operate on anything as delicate as the human eye.*"

We know that an average man would be reduced to a nervous wreck at the prospect of twelve operations on the eye. The entire ordeal taught him acceptance.

Also, it taught him that nothing life could bring him was beyond his strength to endure.

It also taught him that, as John Milton said, "*It is not miserable to be blind. It is only miserable not to endure blindness.*" Also, as Helen

Keller said, "*The only thing worse than being blind is having sight but no vision.*"

As you progress along this journey called life, you will be presented with a lot of unpleasant situations. You discover that you have little or no control over the outcome of many of these situations. They cannot be otherwise. However, you have the choice of either accepting them as inevitable, or adjusting yourself to them, or you can ruin your health and well-being by wallowing in anxiety and worry and possibly ending up a nervous wreck. The prosaic truth is that we all have an in-built capacity to absorb the devastating effects of shock, to endure disaster and tragedy, and then to triumph over them ultimately. Most of us are much more robust than our inner resources being strong enough to see us through if we will only use them. Wise is he who would fully appreciate these profound words of William James, a great philosopher: "*Be willing to have it so. Acceptance of what has happened is the first step to overcoming the consequences of any misfortune.*"

One of the greatest stories ever written about adversity is the book of Job in the Bible. You need to read it and see how a man can get a beating, knocked out and bounce back again.

There is a fifteenth-century cathedral in Amsterdam, Holland that is in ruins. There is an inscription on its walls, written in Flemish, that says, "*It is so. It cannot be otherwise.*"

A vital lesson that all of us will have to learn, eventually, is that we must accept and cooperate with the inevitable. "It is so...it cannot be otherwise." Unfortunately, although understandable, it is not a very easy lesson to learn.

However, it is an enduring truth that even Kings must keep reminding themselves of. King George V framed these words and hung them on the wall of his library at Buckingham Palace: "*Teach me neither to cry for the moon nor over spilt milk.*"

Frankly, circumstances have much less to do with our

happiness or unhappiness than our reaction to those circumstances. If, as the Son of Man declared 2,000 years ago, the kingdom of Heaven is within you frankly, the kingdom of hell is within you also, depending on how you react to the unfortunate circumstances of your life.

No one is immune to the occurrence of disaster and tragedy. Conversely, no one entirely cannot endure disaster and tragedy if they must. Most people think they cannot survive harrowing times when they appear in their life. Most people discover that they are much stronger than they think. Your inner resources are much stronger than you could ever believe until adversity rears its head in your life.

Permit me to make something bright. I am not prescribing that you succumb, with defeat, to all the adversities that come your way. That would be a somewhat fatalistic approach to life, wouldn't it? If the dimmest hope remains that we can redeem a situation, we must put up a good fight.

However, when common sense dictates, we are struggling and railing against something that cannot be otherwise, then we must preserve our sanity by accepting the inevitable.

Nineteen centuries ago, the great philosopher, Epictetus, said, *"There is only one way to happiness, and that is to cease worrying about things are beyond the power of our will."*

The most famous execution and death scene in all human history is the crucifixion of Jesus Christ. Coming a distant second in the annals of man must be the death of Socrates, a great Greek philosopher. Plato rendered what can only pass for an immortal description of the execution, in what must be one of the most moving and poignantly beautiful passages in all literature. After being sentenced to death, on trumped-up charges against him, the rather friendly executioner, on giving Socrates the poison to drink, said: *"Try to bear lightly what needs must be."* Socrates followed this advice. He faced death with calm and composed resignation to the inevitable.

In the turbulent VUCA times and the Fourth Industrial Revolution we now live in, it would amount to nothing short of gross disfavour, both to oneself, and one's organisation, if one did not firmly commit to acceptance of the reality of the times. This total acceptance is what will equip you with the determination to do something proactive about the situation.

COVID – 19 and the massive loses it has inflicted on the world economy is going to be the greatest test of leadership we've ever faced. The fortunes of Amazon, Facebook and other tech giants have increased.

The current climate is turbulent, as leaders of men/women and resources are discovering, with each passing day, all over the world. Things will always go wrong, and the best mindset is to determine to act when they go wrong. You cannot sit on the fence, waiting for some chance and fortunate occurrence to bail you out of your dilemma.

On a final note, we need to examine, even if only briefly, what might be the compelling reason most people entirely cannot accept the reality of situations, especially when such cases present themselves in a glaringly unpleasant light. The most common denominator is a lack of courage. A lack of courage to accept and cooperate with the inevitable, with the attendant need to move out of a comfort zone, may contribute to individual and corporate failure to accept, say, the discomfiting challenges of VUCA-induced chaos and turmoil in an organisation. This is a manifestation of a pervasive fear of the unknown. Courage is not the absence of fear, but the mastery of fear. It is a fear that has helped bury the talents of many men and women, preventing them from achieving their dreams and reaching their true potentials.

Fear and faith may be opposites, since on a most fundamental level, what each of them brings to our lives are also opposites, with anxiety leading to failure, and faith leading to conquest. Your most significant challenge in these turbulent times will be the conquest of fear and the corresponding development of courage. Since anything you practise repeatedly eventually becomes a habit, you can only develop courage by acting courageously anytime courage is called for. A courageous person goes forward despite his fear.

Therefore, the first quality to lead and thrive in today's volatile world is Acceptance - Accepting the fact that we now live in a VUCA world, and the Fourth Industrial Revolution is here to stay.

Let us examine, in pertinent detail, three techniques that great leaders and mentors have successfully employed to weather the bad storms of their private and business lives.

1. *They ponder on what the experience can teach them.*

In the year 1648, poet Robert Herrick wrote in that great literature, 'Hesperides', "*If little labour, little our gains: Man's fate is according to his pains.*"

In 1982, actress Jane Fonda and the exercise company Soloflex simplified this message with: "*No pain, no gain.*"

It is an absolute truism that the people who have learned to look at challenges as valuable teaching moments are the wisest and strongest leaders that we know.

How do they convert pain into personal value?

First, they come into the wholesome comprehension that pain is always a temporary condition and an opportunity to learn. They ask questions like, "How did I get here?" and "What caused this to happen?" Put in quaintly simple terms; they opt for curiosity over self-pity or anger.

The next thing they do is to share their learning and experience with others generously. In summary, they commit to extracting the most out of the opportunity for the benefit of themselves and others.

So, next time you are faced with a challenge, ask yourself what you may stand to learn from it.

2. *Great leaders employ adverse times to reinvent their future.*

"We must reinvent a future free of blinders so that we can choose from real options," so said David Suzuki, an academic and activist.

The choice is the enemy of fear. This is an absolute truism. This is because, when you have a corridor of choices and options, you don't feel trapped by your circumstances. The salient truth is that we all have a myriad of choices, but the most resilient leaders are masters at reminding themselves of this in the face of adversity.

When you face a seemingly adverse situation, start by answering these questions:

- What is the outcome I most want?

- What other outcomes would be useful, as well?

- What stands in my way from making these outcomes happen?

- Who do I know that has overcome similar obstacles to those that stand in my way?

3. *Great leaders resolutely refuse to become furious with their adverse circumstances, but become humorously curious.*

As George Carlin once said, "*Some people see the glass as half full. Others see it half empty. I see a glass that's twice as big as it needs to be.*"

I know someone who loves to exclaim, "Fascinating!" whenever a particularly troubling or unexpected situation arises. What is particularly inspiring to me is that he does so with a laugh, choosing to look at every challenge through the lens of almost child-like curiosity and humour.

I adopt a similar refrain when people ask me, "How's it going?" almost invariably when things are not at their premium best. I laugh and say, "I've never felt more alive!"

What I have discovered is that humour helps you think more broadly and creatively. It is essential for the optimal problem solving, and allows you not to take yourself, or your situation, too seriously.

You might even ask your friends the question, "Can you tell me a few things that are ridiculously funny about this particular problem I am facing?" When they answer, listen for nuggets of truth and wisdom, and avenues for solutions and possibilities you may not have even considered.

I leave you with one last thought.

"I often wonder if the challenge I am so distracted by today is going to make a bit of difference to me when I am old and grey."- Likely not.

Armed with the wisdom of hindsight, I can now see the challenges and obstacles of my life in a new light, as it is with fascinated delight and humble gratitude that I now recognise their inestimable, practical value in my life. This is what I have discovered. Each, and every time I overcame one, I became stronger and better equipped to confront those that were still ahead, very much like a biceps muscle that becomes stronger with constant contractile exertion. To put matters in a nutshell, with each difficulty I had to face, I grew in both mental acuity and emotional stature. Most of all, however, my faith in my ability to surmount the mountain peaks of my life grew exponentially. I am grateful for my problems.

As I trudged along my path, with each passing year, and each passing constellation of experiences, wholesome and adverse, I increasingly came into the near-sublime knowledge that life itself is a project all its own. Also, life is the most challenging project. I also came into the understanding of one indisputable fact. To the perfectly valid degree that anything we gain familiarity with ultimately ends up attracting our contempt, I now found myself in the liberating position of adopting an accommodating stance to the challenging nature of life. I gained intimate familiarity with the fact that experience is challenging. Once I did this, and accepted that fact as a statement of unassailable reality, since familiarity breeds contempt, that life is challenging was no longer one to be celebrated by me, and having been robbed of its mystique, life has become a much easier project to pursue.

CASE STUDY

How Steve Jobs coped with his traumatic exit from Apple

In a nutshell, Steve reframed the situation. Research shows that optimists develop more positive and proactive ways of explaining disappointing events and often reframe them. They see challenges as opportunities. Steve Jobs famously reframed his firing from

Apple. In his Stanford University graduation address, he noted, "*I didn't see it then, but it turned out that getting fired from Apple was the best thing that could have ever happened to me. The lightness of being a beginner again, less sure about everything, replaced the heaviness of being successful. It freed me to enter one of the most creative periods of my life. During the next five years, I started a company named NeXT, another company named Pixar, and fell in love with an amazing woman who would later become my wife. I'm sure none of this would have happened if I hadn't been fired from Apple.*"

This extraordinary entrepreneur adopted an attitude of 'inverse optimism', which proclaimed that the world was, at every turn, conspiring to do him good!

Another example: Mahatma Gandhi's fierce resilience

In the twentieth century, there was no other person who is considered more successful than Mahatma Gandhi. Before his death, he had accomplished nearly all that he had set out to do. To associate failure with Mahatma Gandhi is almost a sacrilege, but his first satyagraha in South Africa, to repeal the registration of Indians, was an utter failure; his political career was over, before it even began. It was then that Mr Naidoo, a close friend, encouraged him to reflect on his actions, and Gandhi realised that the reason for failure was his choice of fellow satyagrahas. These were prosperous merchants and traders who had never experienced hunger or deprivation. A day behind bars was enough to weaken their resolve to support the cause. As a result, Gandhi was forced to settle on a compromise with the white administration, which released them, and his reputation suffered. Gandhi reflected on his mistake, and for the next satyagraha, he chose Indian coal miners. This was a hardy lot who had seen deprivation and would not weaken in prison. The satyagraha was a resounding success, Gandhi's nonviolent protest movement brought him international acclaim, and he never looked back. His resilience enabled him to move forward and transition from 'Gandhi' to Mahatma or 'great soul.' **(Abidi & Joshi, 2015 page)**

Al Siebert (1934 - 2009) who is the bestselling author of the book 'The Survivor Personality: Why Some People are Stronger, Smarter, and More Skilful at Handling Life's Difficulties... and How You Can be, Too', writes that *"The best survivors spend almost no time, especially in emergencies, getting upset about what has been lost, or feeling distressed about things going badly.... For this reason, they rarely take themselves too seriously and are therefore hard to threaten."*

As Jim Rohn tells us in 'The Seasons of Life', *"Life is designed to be a story of achievement despite adversity, not in the absence of adversity, for without adversity achievement could not exist."*

"The world will willingly stand by and let you feel sorry for yourself – until you finally die broke and alone – if that's what you want. It will also stand aside for you once you firmly decide that your present situation is only temporary and that you will get back up and go on to make your mark. The world doesn't have time to care which choice you make, so for yourself at least, give a run at adventure, with your eyes firmly set on achievement, not merely existence and self-pity."

The Dalai Lama's Book of Wisdom says the success of our lives and our future depends on our motivation and determination or self-confidence. Through painful experiences, life sometimes becomes more meaningful. If you look at people who, from the beginning of their lives, have had everything, you may see that when small things happen, they soon lose hope of growing irritated. Other have developed a healthier mental attitude because of their hardship.

Matthew Syed is a former England table tennis champion who has also moved on with great success to a writing and broadcasting career and with some distinction too. His bestselling book, 'Black Box Thinking: The Surprising Truth About Success' concludes that most success follows on from something the rest of us are more intimately familiar with: **failure.**

'Black box thinking', alludes to the data recorders fitted to all aircraft carriers to provide information in case of accidents. Syed's deduction is air travelling has become safer than any other form of travel because of the lessons learned from past failures.

He illustrates his position with the story of United Airlines flight 173 in December 1973, when the flight crew, coming into land, became convinced that the landing gear hadn't locked into place. They spent so long trying to fix the problem they ran out of fuel and had to crash-land in a residential area.

Thanks to the skill of the pilot, and a lot of luck, no one was killed on the ground, and only eight people on the plane lost their lives. But the investigators learned the engineer hadn't been assertive enough in pointing out that fuel was running low. For the pilot, obsessively trying to solve the other problem, time ran out.

After this crash, protocols were put in place, training methods were changed, and nothing like it has happened again. The landing gear was fine, and they could have landed safely.

"The basic proposition of this book," says Syed, *"is that we have an allergic attitude to failure. We try to avoid it, cover it up and airbrush it out of our lives. Instead, we should embrace it and learn from it. That's what Sir James Dyson does, what the Mercedes F1 team does, what Google does, what Sir Dave Brailsford and his British cycling teams do."*

We need to develop resilience to bounce back after each adversity. Karl Weick and Kathleen Sutcliffe in their book 'Managing the Unexpected' (2007) define resilience as the capacity of an organisation to rebound from setbacks or to adjust and find its equilibrium in the face of challenges.

In his book 'The Greatness Guide' (2011), Robin Sharma describes some habits the world's elite adopt in their lives and one habit he mentioned is **using adversity effectively**

But it also reinforces my contention that failure can produce success if you learn from it.

As you move towards your vision, understand that the more you can accept that failure will probably be a part of the process, the more you will use it to your advantage. It fills the political business and entertainment worlds - stories of people who learn from their failures and then fulfilled their dreams. Thomas Jefferson lost to John Adams before he became president. Steve Jobs got tossed out of Apple before returning to revive the company that he founded. Oprah Winfrey lost her role as a newsreader at a Baltimore TV station before getting another shot with a different programme, a talk show that would lead to even bigger things.

Failure is part of the method. Sometimes it comes in waves, sometimes it catches you by surprises. But whatever it hit, understand that it is part of the pursuit. Take something from failure and use it to move your vision along.

That is what we all need to do when adversity strikes; find help, accept help and put them to use. Then, when you're ready, reengage with your vision. That may mean having to reset your game plan and determine new goals. At first, you may find the going tricky. But understand: You won't be the first one to deal with such circumstances. History proved that things could get better.

Credit: The Golden Rules: 10 Steps to World-Class Excellence in Your Life and Work by Bob Bowman, USA Head Swim Coach with Charles Butler

Overcoming adversity

- Face the reality

- Identify the real issues

- Be optimistic

- Right attitude
- Unite the people around the purpose
- Involve others in the solution-generation process
- Turn adversity to advantage

Let me leave you with this quote by Stephen A. Schwarzman, who said in his book 'What It Takes: Lessons in the Pursuit of Excellence', that *"Regardless of how you begin your careers, it is important to realise that your life will not move in a straight line. You recognise that the world is an unpredictable place. Sometimes even gifted people such as yourselves will get knocked back on their heels. You will inevitably confront many difficulties and hardships during your lives. When you face setbacks, you have to dig down and move forward. The resilience you exhibit in the face of adversity – rather than the adversity itself – will be what defines you as a person."*

Summary – Chapter 8

1   Overturning adversity is the hallmark of leadership.

2   Any success story has its fair share of adversity.

3   Adversity can be used by leaders to reinvent themselves

4   Adversities are inevitable, as there are no royal roads to victory

Chapter 9

Audacity
(Attribute 7)

Aword of advice on this chapter. You will gain insights into the lives of leaders who have lived the audacious experience and dared to share these with readers globally. It is my strong belief that these anecdotes will empower and enrich your minds in the quest for audacity.

Audacity in leadership is being bold or daring with disregard to conventional thought or restrictions. Innovative solutions are usually audacious because they break the conventions that exist.

Powerful leaders will step outside of what they know and explore the unknown. They are eager to go after that big idea they are confident will change the world. And they paint a picture of why we should care and help them make it happen.

Take, for instance, the founders of 37 Signals. They solved a problem they had — they weren't happy with the project management software available, so they designed their own. They showed it to their clients and colleagues, who all said they needed it for their business too.

They created an audacious business model, one that rejects most traditional views of successful businesses. Rather than selling to the Fortune 500, they sell to the Fortune 5,000,000

(Source: *ReWork*, by Jason Fried and David Heinemeier Hansson.)

"When my partner and I founded Aperio almost eleven years ago, people said they didn't get it. They saw a chiropractor and an architect and didn't see how we could create a new model for consulting. We dared to believe that our non-traditional backgrounds, expertise in finding simple solutions for complex situations and passionate obsession for helping people and companies optimise their performance would create a better, more effective model for business consulting. Eleven years later, we have consistently and progressively grown, primarily through client referrals, because of our remarkable track record of producing excellent results.

What is your vision? How do you describe it to others? Is it compelling and engaging? Does it break convention? Answering these questions and communicating them well will help you become a more influential leader." – Sandy Nelson, co-founder Aperio International Business Accelerators USA

http://aperiointernational.com/leadership-characteristics-%E2%80%93-part-two/

WHICH AUDACITY ARE YOU?

Steve Farber, the founder of The Extreme Leadership Institute, is a popular keynote speaker and leadership expert. He's the bestselling author of *'The Radical Leap'*, *'The Radical Edge'* and *'Greater Than Yourself.'* In a blog article written in August 2010, he writes:

"My dear friend, Matt Brandt, once described 'audacity' as 'a bold and blatant disregard for normal constraints,' and from that moment on, those words have been emblazoned on my brain.

If you look up the word 'audacious' in Webster's Thesaurus, however, you'll see that it has several very different connotations. One, as it relates to terms like courageous, heroic, and gallant, and another is the audacity synonymous with impudence, temerity, or brazenness.

The difference between the two meanings comes down to love versus ego. Love-inspired audacity is courageous and bold and filled with courage. It's the boldness that's required to change the world for the better.

Ego-inspired audacity is just annoying, irritating, or even–when taken to an extreme–dangerous. Some people are audacious just to draw attention to themselves, grabbing the spotlight, puffing themselves up, or advancing their agenda. They have no care or concern about the impact of their behaviour or action on anyone else. They're not concerned about anything except their image.

And, therefore, they certainly don't qualify for Extreme Leader. Not in my book, anyway.

If you think of yourself as an audacious person–or aspire to be one–I'd encourage you to ask this critical question:

"To do what?"

If your answer falls anywhere south of "to change my piece of the world for the better," you're not there yet. Technically, you may be acting audaciously, but–if I may be blunt–the rest of us will experience you as nothing more than a pain in the patootie. (I've always wanted to use that in a sentence).

So up the ante and raise the stakes. Be bold. Be blatant. Disregard the usual constraints to leave this place better than you found it.

And that's as audacious an intent as I can imagine."

(*Source*: https://www.stevefarber.com/which-audacity-are-you/ Accessed Thursday 23, April 2020)

The motive behind your audacious action must be selfless and not self-serving. Many people are audacious just to impress; that's not noble. You get little accolades for such personal aggrandisement.

Richard Branson: 3 Ways to Be More Audacious in Business

"First, eliminate your fear of failure – and think bigger."

Richard Branson is pretty much audacity in human form. The billionaire English business magnate started as a fresh-faced teenager who was frustrated with the high price of records in his hometown. By making bold choices and never settling for the status quo, Branson built one of the biggest media empires in the world.

He's also started an airline, invested in space tourism, and attempted to circumnavigate the world in a hot-air balloon. He offered three tips for being bold in your own business decisions and channelling your own inner Branson.

1. **Start big.** The initial stage of any project is the hardest. That's why it's so important to take those first steps with confidence. *"The most difficult time is when you're starting from scratch with no financial backing, with just an idea,"* Branson says. *"That is audacious. For somebody like myself, now 40 years on, to do something audacious – it's an awful lot easier than it would have been when I was 15 (just) setting up in business."*

2. **Go all in.** Doing something half-heartedly is the opposite of audacity. Giving your all may be nerve-wracking, but it sets a bold tone that will help propel you forward. *"My feeling is just thrown yourself wholeheartedly into anything you do, and then do it to your utmost and best,"* Branson says. *"You're setting good foundations for the long-term."*

3. **Don't fear failure.** True audacity means taking risks — and with risks comes the potential for disappointment. But don't let that stop you. Branson says he's impressed by *"those people who just have the bravery and the courage to say, 'I see a gap in the market, I see something that's not being done well, I'm gonna give it a go. Even though I may fall flat on my face and it might cost me everything.' Now that's audacious."*

Branson is the epitome of being audacious. No wonder, he wins big. When audacity aims to improve and break new grounds. It should be respected and encouraged.

(Source: https://www.inc.com/rachel-monroe/richard-branson-how-to-be-more-audacious.html *Accessed Thursday 23, April 2020)*

Cantor Fitzgerald's Howard William Lutnick - A leader with audacity

Julia La Roche, writing in the online journal of Business Insider edition of September 11, 2011 illustrates 'The Amazing and Heartbreaking Story of The CEO Who Lived and Rebuilt His Firm After 9/11: Howard Lutnick.' It's an audacious story worth re-telling.

"Perhaps the only reason Cantor Fitzgerald's chief executive Howard W. Lutnick didn't perish during the September 11, 2001 terrorist attacks on the World Trade Centre is thanks to his young son.

That Tuesday morning was the day his five-year-old son Kyle started kindergarten. He and his wife both wanted to take him to his first day at Horace Mann School.

Lutnick was in his son's classroom when he first heard the news of the attacks that would forever change his life and his firm. Cantor Fitzgerald occupied the 101st to the 105th floors of One World Trade Centre — just above the impact zone of the hijacked plane.

Cantor Fitzgerald suffered the most significant loss of life of any company. The firm lost 658 of its 960 employees, almost two-thirds of its workforce.

What's even more heart-breaking, Cantor Fitzgerald had a policy of hiring relatives, so those who lost someone at the firm likely lost over one loved one. Lutnick lost his brother.

Because the attacks had devastated Cantor Fitzgerald so severely, the firm was not expected to survive. Remarkably, within a week, the firm got its trading back online.

And Lutnick committed to keeping Cantor Fitzgerald going, despite the odds and the difficult choices that had to be made. Lutnick made the controversial decision to cut off the paychecks to employees who were killed. Instead, he gave the victim's families 25% of the firm's profits for five years, and ten years of health insurance. He's been trying to fulfil his vow to keep the firm alive for the last decade.

Cantor Fitzgerald suffered a tremendous loss, but it might also be one of the greatest comeback stories on Wall Street. Today, Cantor Fitzgerald operates in its Midtown offices at 499 Park Avenue. The new offices are located on the second floor, hundreds of floors below the firm's position in the World Trade Centre.

With the 10th anniversary of the attacks, Lutnick admits the memory of that day still haunts him. He recently recalled a dream in an interview with The New York Post."

Barack Obama's book, ***Audacity of Hope*** is an inspiration. His life shows how it is to be audacious, having become the first African-American President of the United States. Audacious folks inspire us to aspire. They give hope and rekindle our desire to fight back, even when we have no inherent power to do so.

I recently read an article in the summer 2020 edition of Harvard Business Review. The article titled "Layoffs That Don't Break Your Company" was originally published in the May-June 2018 edition by Sandra J. Sucher **and** Shalene Gupta

Two great forces are transforming the very nature of work: automation and ever fiercer global competition. To keep up, many organizations have had to rethink their workforce strategies, often making changes that are disruptive and painful. Typically, they turn to episodic restructuring and routine layoffs, but in the long term both damage employee engagement and company profitability. Some companies, however, have realized that they need a new approach.

Consider the case of Nokia. At the beginning of 2008 senior managers at the Finnish telecom firm were celebrating a one-year 67% increase in profits. Yet competition from low-cost Asian competitors had driven Nokia's prices down by 35% over just a few years. Meanwhile, labour costs in Nokia's Bochum plant in Germany had risen by 20%. For management, the choice was clear: Bochum had to go. Juha Äkräs, Nokia's senior vice president of human resources at the time, flew in to talk about the layoff with the plant's 2,300 employees. As he addressed them, the crowd grew more and more agitated. "It was a totally hostile situation," he recalls.

The anger spread. A week later 15,000 people protested at Bochum. German government officials launched an investigation and demanded that Nokia pay back subsidies it had received for the plant. Unions called for a boycott of Nokia products. The news was filled with pictures of crying employees and protesters crushing Nokia phones. Ultimately, the shutdown cost Nokia €200 million — more than €80,000 per laid-off employee — not including the ripple effects of the boycott and bad press. The firm's market share in Germany plunged; company managers estimate that from 2008 to 2010 Nokia lost €700 million in sales and €100 million in profits there.

In 2011, when Nokia's mobile phone business tanked, its senior leaders decided they needed to restructure again. That would involve laying off 18,000 employees across 13 countries over the next two years. Chastened by their experience in Germany, Nokia's executives were determined to find a better solution. This time, Nokia implemented a program that sought to ensure that employees felt the process was equitable and those who were laid off had a soft landing.

One of us, Sandra, has spent eight years researching best practices for workforce change in global multinational companies. She has seen that all too frequently companies do bad layoffs, do layoffs for the wrong reason, or worse, do both. By "bad," we mean layoffs that aren't fair or perceived as fair by employees and that have lasting negative knock-on effects. The job cuts in Bochum ignited outrage because Nokia had generated so much profit the year before. Consequently, they were seen as unjust and took a steep toll on Nokia's reputation and sales. And when we say "wrong reasons," we mean done to achieve short-term cost cuts instead of long-term strategic change. In 2008, Nokia did have the right reasons, but it still suffered because of its process.

Some governments, recognizing the massive damage layoffs create, have written laws protecting employees against them. For example, several European countries require companies to provide a social or economic justification before they can conduct layoffs. France, however, recently eliminated the requirement to provide an economic justification, and in the United States companies can conduct layoffs at will. Regardless of how easy it might be to cut personnel; executives should remember that doing so will have consequences.

The research clearly shows that bad layoffs and layoffs for the wrong reasons rarely help senior leaders accomplish their goals. In this article, we'll present a better approach to workforce transitions — one that makes sparing use of staff reductions and ensures that when they do happen, the process feels fair and the company and the affected parties are set up for success.

Let's look again at what happened at Nokia in 2011, when its senior leaders realized the company needed another restructuring. Then-chairman **Jorma Ollila** was determined to avoid another Bochum. To help the company do so, a small team of senior leaders developed Nokia's Bridge program, which aimed to see that as many employees as possible had a new opportunity lined up the day their current job ended. Nokia opened Bridge centres in the 13 countries where the layoffs would take place. The program outlined five paths employees could choose from:

1. Find another job at Nokia.

In order to avoid favouritism, selection committees were formed to determine which employees to retain, instead of having local managers choose.

2. Find another job outside Nokia.

The centres offered outplacement services, including career coaching, résumé workshops, career fairs, and networking events.

3. Start a new business.

Individual employees or teams could present business proposals to win grants of up to €25,000. Employees were given two months to develop their plans, as well as support such as coaching and mentoring, networking introductions, and training. Nokia took no stake in any of the funded businesses.

4.   Learn something new.

Nokia offered training grants for business-management and

trade-school courses in many areas, including restaurant management, cosmetology, construction, and firefighting.

5. Build a new path.

The company offered financial support to employees who had personal goals they wanted to accomplish, such as volunteering.

Nokia spent €50 million on Bridge, or about €2,800 per employee. That accounted for just 4% of the €1.35 billion it spent on restructuring from 2011 to 2013. As a result of the program, 60% of the 18,000 affected workers knew their next step the day their jobs ended. Overall, 85% of the Finnish Bridge participants said they were satisfied with the program, while 67% of global employees said they were. Furthermore, the layoff candidates and the remaining employees maintained or improved quality levels throughout the restructuring. Employees at the sites that were targeted for downsizing achieved €3.4 billion in new-product revenues, one-third of new-product sales – the same proportion they had brought in before. Employee engagement scores in all areas of the company held steady throughout the restructuring. And, unlike the situation in Bochum, there were no labour actions of any kind in the 13 countries where the layoffs happened. By all accounts Nokia had indeed found a better approach to workforce change.

In 2017, three years after selling its devices and services business to Microsoft, Nokia used an enhanced version of the Bridge program to handle its latest restructuring. Microsoft Finland has rolled out a similar program. And Finland's government has even taken cues from Bridge and incorporated ideas from it into legislation outlining what companies that conduct layoffs are required to provide for affected employees.

CONCLUSION

One of the biggest questions organizations face as they grapple with a constantly shifting economic landscape is whether their current workforce can help them make the transitions necessary to their success. While companies tend to prioritize short-term financial results over the long-term well-being of their employees, employees are the lifeblood that enables a company to keep delivering the products and services that ultimately generate shareholder benefits. Michelin's and Nokia's experiences show that employees can and should be trusted to perform well, even when they know they might lose their jobs. For all companies, planning thoughtful workforce change instead of automatically resorting to layoffs is a better way to address the vicissitudes of technological transformation and intensifying competition.

A version of this article appeared in the May–June 2018 issue (pp.122–129) of *Harvard Business Review*.

Sandra J. Sucher **is the Joseph L. Rice, III, Faculty Fellow and a professor of management practice at Harvard Business School. She is the co-author of the forthcoming book** *Trusted: How Companies Build It, Lose It, and Regain It.*

Shalene Gupta **is a research associate at Harvard Business School. She is the co-author of the forthcoming book** *Trusted: How Companies Build It, Lose It, and Regain It.*

The above shows that you can be audacious at the same time be compassionate especially when undergoing restructure just like what **Jorma Ollila above did in Nokia**

Summary – Chapter 9

1   All great leaders are audacious.

2   To be audacious is good only if it is not self-serving.

3   Any audacious action must be big, bold and impactful, to be
    of any significance

Chapter 10

Conclusion

Having established 'The top 7 Attributes Essential for Leading in a VUCA World,' we can now summarily declare that the rate of change in the business world today is proving to be far greater than our ability to respond. In a world that is now described as VUCA (Volatile, Uncertain, Complex and Ambiguous), there are major tectonic shifts that demand a new mindset of leadership. First, let us look at these shifts.

In recent years, we have seen the disruption of market leaders like Kodak and Nokia amongst many others. The average lifespan of a Fortune 500 company has gone down from 67 years in 1937 to 18 years in 2011. With advances in technology, mobile devices have replaced so many traditional utilities: calculators, alarm clocks and small digital cameras. Generations at the workplace as we used to know it are changing, and new generations are bringing different values, expectations and mindsets at work. The rise in automation is resulting in massive disruption. Right from purchasing items to booking taxis, and filing tax returns, everything increasingly becomes automated. The agents, intermediaries and the whole supply chain related to these services have been disrupted. And, we are not even talking about automated automobiles, which may yet turn out to be the next big frontier for the technology battle.

With a hyper-connected workforce, organisational cultures are becoming more and more transparent. With opportunities abounding at every corner, employees are becoming more of 'volunteers' who have global choices. In this 'new normal', having a compelling purpose is a mandatory pre-requisite for profits to follow. Traditional hierarchical structures are being dismantled to give way to purposeful networks and communities of people working together to achieve a shared purpose. The cumulative impact of these forces demands a new mindset and competencies for leaders to stay relevant and make a positive difference to people and businesses.

If you are a leader at any level in a modern organisation or aspiring to be one, here are some critical competencies and skills you will need to thrive in a VUCA world.

1. Have a Vision

Vision is a constant force. It is a critical anchor that drives decisions, actions and judgments. With a younger workforce that is purpose-driven, having a compelling vision for the future is also a key driver of engaging and retaining high-performing team members. A compelling vision is an essential pre-requisite for any community or network to succeed. Leaders who will thrive in a VUCA future are the ones who have a clear vision of where they want their organisations and teams to be.

2. Embrace an Abundance Mindset

An abundance mindset sees possibilities, while a constraint mindset sees challenges. A leader's ability to spot the white spaces, unique problems and interdisciplinary intersections is as critical in the new world order as the ability to 'do something about it.' In a VUCA world, leaders must listen to the future because of continually scanning the horizon, being future-oriented and having a strategic foresight without losing sight of the current reality. When they do this, leaders develop a unique ability to see through the contradictions of the future others cannot see.

3. Weave Ecosystems for Human Engagement

One of the biggest leadership challenges is creating an environment that taps into the intrinsic motivation of people. Deloitte's Human Capital Trends 2015 reports that softer areas such as culture, engagement, leadership and development have become the urgent priorities on a CEO's desk. We create an ecosystem of human

involvement when leaders understand the primary
drivers of human engagement. These are the need for
trust, the need to have hope, the need to feel a sense of
worth and the need to feel competent. When most
'engagement initiatives' are aimed at providing external
motivation, we need leaders who can build trust
through integrity and results, who can mentor and
coach others, who can clarify the meaning of the work
people do and then go-ahead to build a positive
influence.

4. Anticipate and Create Change

When changes around us are constant and rapid, leaders
must use the wisdom from their future-mindedness and
strategic foresight to 'create change' before an external
change forces them to react. When leaders ride the wave
of changes, they must involve people in the change
process, prioritise what's important and execute changes
in smaller capsules. Leaders nurture change by
maintaining a comfortable balance between the needs of
the context, the needs of others and their own needs.

5. Be an Agile Learner

Rapidly changing context is like a treadmill that compels
leaders to learn continuously in a self-directed mode.
Leaders must be always curious and carry a 'beginner's
mind' which is also willing to give up on conventional
approaches. We can call this unlearning. Leaders need

meta-cognition and awareness of the bigger picture. When thrown into unfamiliar situations, leaders need to learn from those experiences.

6. *Network and Collaborate*

To make sense of the changing trends, practices and expectations, leaders in today's world need to collaborate relentlessly within and outside the organisation. A social mindset will enable leaders to create, engage with and nurture purposeful business and social networks through social media and interpersonal communication. Apple and Microsoft were sworn enemies, just like Coca-Cola and Pepsi. But when Jobs took over the company again in 1997, it had been losing money for 12 years. So, what did Steve Jobs do? He approached Bill Gates and what followed was a $150 million investment into Apple. That enabled Apple to achieve financial stability finally. Both companies ended up winners when they previously had been fierce competitors.

7. *Relentlessly Focus on the Customer*

Customer-centric is a way of doing business with your **customer** in a way that provides a positive **customer** experience before and after the sale to drive repeat business, **customer** loyalty and profits. Customer-centricity is and will always remain at the heart of effective leadership. Helping customers navigate through the changes is as critical for leaders as it is to steer their organisations effectively. Customer-centric leaders truly 'listen' to the voice of their customers, engage them at a profound level, and build long-term relationships by adding substantial value to their customers.

8. Develop People

Leadership in the new world goes far beyond external tags and titles. It is about attending effectively to the needs of the stakeholders, the most important ones being the people who make things work. Leaders, in this VUCA world, have to model the behaviours they seek to help people in building their skill set and attitude, create learning forums, design work that will directly exploit the real potential and lead through their influence, and not through their authority. The primary task and obligation of a leader are to build more and future leaders.

9. Design for the Future

Leaders are designers of systems for the future. They do so by building an emotional infrastructure, organisational structures, methods and processes. If organisations are purposeful networks of people, leaders need a compelling purpose that people in the organisation can share. Leaders will have to pay equal attention to leveraging diversity and drawing on multiple points of views and experiences.

10. Constantly Clarify and Communicate

When working with a global workforce, leaders will need the ability to communicate effectively across cultures. Like a location pointer on a GPS map, leaders must clarify the current situation concerning changing external demands continually. Equally crucial for leaders is to reiterate and reinforce vision, values and strategies. Finally, leaders have to help others in clarifying the meaning of their work, communication and clarity being the currencies of effective leadership. In his book, 'Leading Change', John P Kotter said, "*Great visions are nothing if they cannot be communicated. Thus, the use of story/metaphor, multiple media (/people), simplicity and repetition, and leading by example all apply.*"

Summary – Chapter 11

1 In the light of the COVID – 19 Pandemic, the world economy is going to experience a directional shift. Already, many businesses are collapsing because of low patronage. This, in turn, has resulted in massive lay-offs. The application of VUCA principles to the realities would help leaders navigate out of the present storm.

2 Trust weighs heavily on accountable and transparent leadership.

3 Ethical morality cannot be divorced from true leadership

Chapter 11

Last words

VUCA calls out to us to get out of our comfort zone. VUCA is a condition that calls for a lot of questions. These are penetrating questions that ferret out many nuances and possibilities. These are questions that stimulate differing views and debate. They are open-ended questions that fuel the imagination. They are also analytical questions that distinguish what we think from what we know. Almost invariably, the only thing you know with certainty about your strategy is that it's wrong. Only persistent probing will help you discern if your strategy is off by 5 percent or 95 percent before events swiftly reveal the answer to you. That is why agility is critical. Agility is vital because strategic adjustments must be made continually.

VUCA is a condition that calls for many penetrating, challenging, open-ended and analytical questions. Yet, the complexity in VUCA centres on the dynamic relationships in which similar inputs may yield different outputs. It is critical to know which forces are positive, which are negative, and which could proceed either way. Continually asking questions will help you see patterns and make more accurate predictions. As a leader, you must encourage open and direct feedback, and ideas that challenge the status quo.

A good leader should try to create an oasis of certainty amid VUCA turbulence. Unfortunately, constant change can set people on edge because human beings crave certainty. People worry about their jobs, status, and influence. This can hurt engagement, productivity, and the willingness to act independently. But a good and responsive leader can reassure his team through stability and transparency of the process. For example, you can insist on being clear about your decision-making criteria and remain consistent in applying them. Clarify that you will accommodate learning-based mistakes inevitable in a fast-changing environment and be sure to capture what you learn as a way of certifying and validating its value. Think about these failures as a resource you've paid for upfront. Finally, remain firmly grounded on the foundation of your values. They should endure, drive decision making and action, and be enthusiastically and energetically celebrated to give them high visibility amid the hurly-burly of daily work.

Ensure the avoidance of additional and unnecessary turbulence. For example, rather than having regular anxiety-inducing reorganisations of your hierarchy, activities that rapidly become outdated, strike out for a more flexible, minimalist structure complemented by skills such as effective team building, that create fluidity and the expectation that structures will evolve.

VUCA isn't something to be solved. VUCA is VUCA. Attempts to simplify complexity, or to break volatility, uncertainty, and ambiguity down into smaller and smaller parts hoping each can be decoded and countered will not make them go away. This is because there are too many elements beyond the control of traditional centres of power and authority. It is a network phenomenon and cannot be mastered through industrial age structures and practices. Insist on attending on time to how your organisation responds to issues of volatility, uncertainty, complexity, and ambiguity because the world is getting more and more VUCA every single day.

Conclusively, here are a few practical suggestions for serving the VUCA times.

Talent development and succession planning will be critical requirements of the leaders of the future. Leaders will have to help develop their future replacements, in particular, by giving up-and-coming leaders opportunities to develop skills such as emotional intelligence, influence, and compassion. The general conclusion is that, given the ongoing complexity and changing nature of the role of leadership, broad training in a more classic format, for instance, growing up in a series of positions with increasing responsibility, is only a small part of the preparation required.

The characteristics of leadership will require candidates who are less rigid and more flexible. A leader must very quickly have a change of lens and must be able to use lenses that can zoom in and out quickly, and with this put himself in the right place with the right attitude.

The ability to accept and drive change will be necessary, as will develop a heightened comfort level with ambiguity and uncertainty. If you're afraid of change, you're missing the opportunity to grow, and you're missing the opportunity to create more significant innovation and creativity in your organisation. Leaders of tomorrow should recognise that change is an opportunity and should have the courage and desire to work with their teams to bring it about.

Leaders must become comfortable with change, be curious, collaborate, be adaptable, have a purpose, and seek balance. They must become comfortable working and drawing opinions from a diverse array of individuals. They must create a sense of teamwork by communicating to people that their ideas are essential. Leaders must learn how to take thoughtful risks and be willing to fail.

The conduct and performance of leaders affect everyone: employees, investors, consumers. Future leaders, therefore, need to embrace the responsibility of taking into consideration a multitude of accountabilities and societal expectations. They must put the interest of others ahead of theirs. They must put themselves to the service of society.

What separates ordinary people from extraordinary people is that little extra. When you decide today to download my new book and apply what you learn in the book, you will become an extraordinary person, and that is who you are. I challenge you to become one because you can. I think the writer and mountain climber James Ullman summed it all up when he said something like: "*Challenge is the core and mainspring of all human action. If there's an ocean, we cross it. If there's a disease, we cure it. If there's a wrong, we right it. If there's a record, we break it. And if there's a mountain, we climb it.*"

You can start at the bottom and rise to the top. You can turn nothing into something. You can turn pennies into fortune and disaster into success. You've Got the Power! To create magic in all areas of your life because YOU ARE A UNIQUE AND MASTERPIECE CREATION. You have a unique talent, skills and capabilities. You have a unique voiceprint, palm print, footprint and fingerprint. You have a unique destiny that only you can fulfil. You have a unique history and never in the world's history has someone like you existed. You have a unique genetic code. You have a unique DNA. It is even suggested that your DNA carries with it the wisdom of previous generations. Above all, you are endowed with the seeds of greatness. YOU'VE GOT THE POWER!

You must use this power, however, to create a better future for yourself and others. Development is what this world needs and it is our collective responsibility to contribute our quota within our little space.

Nobody says it is going to be easy. Indeed, there are no easy choices and things are going to get tougher. But remember, when the going gets tough, the tough get going.

Chapter 12

A Message for Africa

Over recent years, Africa's the moral conscience of the world, and the least developed of its six continents has witnessed a mini-revival. Several nations have gradually diversified their economies, and the World Bank expects that most African countries will reach middle-income status, defined as at least $1,000 per person a year by 2025 if current growth rates continue.

Over the last decade, growth in Africa has surpassed that of East Asia and statistics reveal that parts of the continent are now enjoying the sale of raw materials, economic diversification and increasing political stability. According to the World Bank, the economy of Sub-Saharan African countries grew at rates that match or surpass global rates over the last ten years.

Some economies that have experienced the most above the global average over the last decade include Mauritania with growth at 19.8%, Angola with 17.6%, Mozambique with 7.9% and Malawi with 7.8%. Other fast growers include Chad, Ethiopia and

Nigeria, while annual Gross Domestic Product (GDP) growth has averaged about 6% a year.

Ethiopia, Africa's second-most populous nation, has been a particular success story as it is gradually transitioning from an agrarian society to one that provides services. Ethiopian Airlines has established itself as Africa's most successful carrier and the country's capital, Addis Ababa, now has an urban metro network, which compares with anything that exists in the developed world.

As recently as 2014, Ethiopia was recording 10% annual GDP growth rates, and although this has slowed down a bit, the country still has one of the fastest-growing economies in the world. This is because of introducing economic reforms that have resulted in many properties owned by the government being privatised.

Almost 50% of Ethiopia's population is under 18, and even though educational enrolment at primary and tertiary level has increased significantly, job creation has not caught up with the increased production of graduates. As at 2015, agriculture accounted for almost 40.5% of GDP, 81% of exports and 85% of the labour force and many other economic activities depend on agriculture, including marketing, processing and shipping.

Now, however, there are plans to diversify into other sectors including telecommunications, mining, energy, manufacturing, transport, telecommunications and tourism. With a gross domestic product of $170bn, Ethiopia is Africa's seventh-largest economy behind Nigeria, South Africa, Egypt, Algeria, Morocco and Angola.

Leading the pack is the continent's giant Nigeria with a GDP of about $550bn, a population of 188m and until recently, one of the fastest-growing economies in the world. Nigeria is the world's 22nd largest economy, its sixth biggest agricultural producer, number six in terms of crude oil exports and the seventh most populous nation on earth.

According to a Citigroup report published in February 2011, Nigeria will get the highest average GDP growth in the world between 2010 and 2050. One of the significant sources of investment in the country is remittances from its large diaspora who send back home $35bn a year.

Nigeria's foreign economic relations revolve around its role in supplying the world economy with oil and natural gas, as the country looks to diversify its exports, harmonise and encourage foreign direct investment. In October 2005, Nigeria implemented the Economic Community for the West African States (ECOWAS) standard external tariff, which reduced the number of tariff bands applicable.

Before this revision, import tariffs constituted Nigeria's second-largest source of revenue after crude oil exports. In 2005, Nigeria achieved a significant breakthrough when it agreed with the Paris Club to eliminate its debts through a combination of write-downs and buybacks. Since then, the debt to GDP ratio has been very low.

Of late, Nigeria has suffered from the impact of falling crude oil prices as crude now sells for about $50 a barrel compared with over $100 a barrel about three years ago. Also, militancy in the oil-producing Niger Delta has cut output over the last two years to below 2m barrels from a high of 2.7m barrels a day.

Mauritania, Africa's fastest-growing economy has extensive deposits of iron ore, which account for almost 50% of total exports. With the current rise in metal prices, gold and copper mining companies are opening mines in the country's interior, creating jobs and boosting economic activity.

Besides, the nation's coastal waters are among the most productive fishing areas in the world, with a wide variety of stock available. Mauritania is also a significant oil producer with the

Chinguetti offshore oil project discovered in 2001 has proven reserves of about 120m barrels of crude.

Botswana is another major African success story, which has had the highest average economic growth rate in the world, averaging about 9% per year between 1966 and 1999. Growth in private sector employment has averaged about 10% a year over the first 30 years of independence.

Over the years, Botswana's economic record has been built on a combination of diamond mining, prudent fiscal policies, international financial and technical assistance and cautious foreign policy. It also rates as the least corrupt country in Africa by Transparency International.

By one estimate, Botswana has the fourth-highest gross national income at purchasing power parity in Africa, giving it a standard of living like that of Mexico and Turkey. Tourism is an increasingly important industry in the country, accounting for almost 12% of GDP as Botswana not only offers excellent game viewing and birding but is also home to one of the largest herds of free-ranging elephants in the world.

Botswana's Central Kalahari Game Reserve also offers some of the most remote and unspoiled wilderness in southern Africa. Several national parks and game reserves, with their abundant wildlife and wetlands, are major tourist attractions thanks to the abundant presence of animals like lions, hyenas, cheetahs, leopards, wild dogs and antelope.

Angola remains one of the fastest-growing economies in the world, enjoying an annual average GDP growth of 11.1% between 2001 and 2010. Unfortunately, Angola was plagued with a bitter 27-year civil war after independence in 1975, which lasted until 2002, and economic recovery has only begun over the last 15 years.

Despite extensive oil and gas resources, diamonds, hydroelectric power, potential fertile agricultural land and a large population, about a third of the population relies on subsistence agriculture. This has mainly been down to the effects of the civil war, but now that the nation has peace, the government has developed its infrastructure and diversify the economy.

Like Nigeria, however, Angola too overly depends on crude oil for its survival as the sector accounts for over 50% of GDP, over 90% of export revenue and over 80% of government income. Also, like Nigeria, corruption and public-sector mismanagement problems have combined to stifle economic growth and diversification.

Mozambique is another country that has only begun enjoying economic growth since the end of its civil war that lasted between 1977 and 1992. In 1987, the government embarked on a series of macroeconomic reforms designed to stabilise the economy, and it is only over the last 30 years that they have yielded dividends.

Inflation was brought to single digits during the late 1990s and fiscal reforms, including the introduction of a value-added tax and a review of the customs service, have improved the government's revenue collection abilities. A combination of increased revenue from crude oil, mining, manufacturing, tourism, agriculture and telecommunications have led to increased GDP growth rates.

Mozambique's average growth rate between 1993 and 1999 was 6.7%, and from 1997 to 1999, it averaged over 10% per year. Over 1,200 state-owned enterprises have been privatised by the government and preparations for further liberalisation are underway for the remaining parastatals, including those in the telecommunications, electricity, water service, aviation, ports, and railway sectors.

As part of this reform programme, the government frequently selects a strategic foreign investor when privatising a parastatal. In the mid-1990s, the World Bank made it necessary for Mozambique to liberalise its cashew sector, which resulted in the lifting of protectionist measures to increase the incomes of farmers.

Like Mozambique, its neighbour Malawi is predominantly agricultural, with about 90% of the population living in rural areas. However, despite this, reforms have sought to address the problem by diversifying the economy, lifting many trade restrictions, privatising state parastatals and removing tariffs.

In 2013, agriculture accounted for 27% of Malawi's GDP, over 80% of the labour force and about 80% of all exports. Until now, Malawi's most famous export crop is tobacco, which accounted for half of the export revenue in 2012 and this has presented a problem as the global drive to limit cigarette consumption has struck.

Malawi's dependence on tobacco is growing; as being the world's number 10 producer, the product accounts for about 70% of export revenue. In addition, Malawi also relies heavily on tea, sugarcane and coffee, with these three plus tobacco making up over 90% of export revenue.

Given the realities of the current harsh global economic climate, African countries must be more competitive. As of now, they are still mainly suppliers of primary products like crude oil, solid minerals and cash crops and with the volatility on the world market, they live at the mercy of international prices.

Several nations have realised this and are now moving to diversify their economies, add value to their products and introduce private competition into production. As a continent, Africa must continue with this and come up with a survival plan aimed at making her competitive in the global marketplace.

My Top 10 Tips on How Africa Counties Can Survive in the Current Harsh Economic Climate

i.   Diversify your economy

ii. Add value to whatever it is you produce

iii. Liberalise your economy and allow private competition

iv. States should stop paying subsidies to producers like farmers

v.   Never rely on one product for revenue as its price could collapse any time

vi. Make generating taxation revenue a key policy objective. As a principle, aim for a tax-to-GDP ratio of about 30%

vii. Get manufacturers to locate factories in your economies where they will process goods for domestic consumption and export

viii. Reduce high inflationary tariffs that make imports unnecessarily expensive

ix. Make services such as tourism, telecommunications, banking and finance an integral part of your economy

x.   Invest in infrastructure as it cuts manufacturing costs, makes your economy more attractive to investors and increases the scope for diversification.

African countries must enthrone transparent and patriotic leaders without which the nations in that continent would not enjoy the stability needed to drive the economies.

- APPENDICES -

*How to fast-track your leadership development (Top 12 Tips)

1) Invest in yourself—Keep Learning

To fast track your leadership development and have a competitive edge in the commercial world, you must invest in yourself.

In these highly competitive times, people are constantly upgrading and updating their training and knowledge in every field. Therefore, you need to invest in yourself properly to grow your leadership skill.

Spend on courses, seminars, conferences for your development and the betterment of your ability to serve others. There is a correlation between learning and earning. The more you learn, the more you earn. It is said that one fundamental way of determining how capable an individual will be is the rate at which the person comes up with new and innovative ideas/strategies to handle life's complicated issues both at work and otherwise.

I attend a minimum of three conferences a year. In leadership, business and human resources.

A Chinese proverb says *"Learning is a treasure that will follow its owner everywhere."*

Sustainable skill and competency development are the key to innovativeness and increased productivity, which is critical to performance and bottom-line.

The best way to prove that you believe in yourself is to invest in yourself. That's the proper thing to do, before you even ask for the support of others.

2). Leaders Are Readers.
Read good books on leadership

According to Tony Onyemaechi Elumelu, a Nigerian economist, entrepreneur, and philanthropist who is the Chairman of *Heirs Holdings*, the *United Bank for Africa, TRANSCORP* and founder of *The Tony Elumelu Foundation, "Voracious reading is the solution to making a difference. Knowledge increases confidence, and confidence is a key attribute for excellence."*

Brian Tracy said, *"Read in your field 30-60 minutes each day. This will translate into one book per week, 50 books per year."*

Bill Gates reads about 50 books per year, which breaks down to 1 per week. Mark Zuckerberg resolved to read a book every two weeks throughout 2015.

Oprah Winfrey selects one of her favourite books every month for her Book Club members to read and discuss.

Matthew Ashimolowo, Founder and Senior Pastor of London-based Kingsway International Christian Centre (KICC), said, "*I read two books a week, that's eight books a month and 96 a year.*"

I read 48 books a year which breaks down to 4 books a month.

Below are some leadership books that have impacted my life the most:

i.   *The 7 Habits of Highly Effective People* by Stephen Covey

ii.   *On becoming a Leader* by Warren Bennis

iii.   *The 21 Irrefutable Laws of Leadership* by John Maxwell

iv.   *Leaders Eat Last* by Simon Sinek

v.   *Start with Why* by Simon Sinek

vi.   *Leadership: Theory and Practice* by Peter G. Northouse

vii.   *The Spirit of Leadership* Dr Myles Munroe

viii. *Authentic Leadership: Rediscovering the Secrets to Creating Lasting Value* by Bill George and Pfeiffer Wiley

ix.   *Leading Out Loud: Inspiring Change through Authentic Communication* by Terry Pearce and Jossey Bass Wiley

x.   *Awakening the Leader Within: A Journey to Authenticity and Purpose* by Kevin Cashman, Jack Forem, John Wiley & Sons Inc

xi.   *True North: Discover Your Authentic Leadership (JB Warren Bennis Series)* by David Gergen

xii.   **Identity Leadership: To Lead Others You Must First Lead Yourself** by Stedman Graham

xiii. *Finding your True North* by Bill George, Andrew McLean and Nick Craig

xiv.   *Why Should Anyone Be Led by You? What It Takes to*

Be an Authentic Leader by Rob Goffee and Gareth Jones.

xv.   *Talk Like TED: The 9 Public-Speaking Secrets of the World's Top Minds* by Carmine Gallo

xvi.   *Good to Great: Why Some Companies Make the Leap and Others Don't* by Jim Collins

xvii.   *Developing the Leader Within You developing* by John C. Maxwell

xviii.   *Man's Search for Meaning* by Viktor E. Frankl

xix.   *5 Levels of Leadership* by John Maxwell

xx.   *Drive* by Daniel H. Pink

xxi.   *How to Win Friends and Influence People* by Dale Carnegie

xxii.   *Disruptive. Think Epic. Be Epic: 25 Successful Habits for An Extremely Disruptive World* by Bill Jensen

xxiii.   *Leading Without a Title* by Timothy Yao

xxiv.   *Learning to Lead: The Journey to Leading Yourself, Leading Others, and Leading an Organization* by Ron Williams with Karl Weber

xxv.   *The Art of War* by Sun Tzu

xxvi.   *Start with Why: How Great Leaders Inspire Everyone to Take Action* by Simon Sinek

xxvii.   *Execution: The Discipline of Getting Things Done* by Larry Bossidy & Ram Charan

xxviii.   *Leading Change* by John Kotter

xxix.   *Thinking, Fast and Slow* by Daniel Kahneman

xxx.   *The Five Dysfunctions of a Team: A Leadership Fable* by Patrick Lencioni *xxxi.*   *Effective Leadership: A Self-development Manual Book* by John Adair

xxxii.   *The 21 Irrefutable Laws of Leadership: Follow Them and People Will Follow You* by John C. Maxwell

xxxiii.   *Primal Leadership: Unleashing the Power of Emotional Intelligence* by Daniel Goleman, Richard Boyatzis & Annie McKee

xxxiv.   *Good to Great: Why Some Companies Make the Leap ... and Others Don't* by Jim Collins

xxxv.   *Wooden on Leadership* by John Wooden & Steve Jamison

xxxvi.   *Developing the Leader Within You 2.0 and Leadershift,* both by John C. Maxwell

xxxvii.   *Leading in the Next Normal: A Guide to Building an Engaged, Resilient and Agile Virtual Workforce* by R Michael Anderson

xxxviii.   *Leading with Cultural Intelligence: The Real Secret to Success* by David Livermore

xxxix.   *Leading Without Authority* by Keith Ferrazzi

xl.   *Identity Leadership: To Lead Others You Must First Lead Yourself* by Stedman Graham

Which book/books do you plan to read this month? Write it now....

Reading is to the mind, what focus is to the body. You must read beyond your field. Read, write, but master your area of speciality by reading the best books on the subject. That's how to stay current.

3). *Volunteering*

Volunteering is another great way to fast track your leadership development. Volunteering, according to NCVO () is someone spending time, unpaid, doing something that aims to benefit the environment or someone who they're not closely related to.

Volunteering in the community is one of the things that assisted in my leadership development.

You can volunteer in your local community, your place of worship or in your organisation.

I have volunteered as a career development coach with Shaw Trust where I provided coaching on interview skills, goal setting, self-development, confidence and motivation building to those seeking employment.

I was also a Business Mentor with Start-up Loan, where I mentored those who are starting in business. I was a school governor for four years in my daughter's primary school, and I chaired the personal committee. While in this role, I developed my strategic leadership and excellent governance skills.

In the Nigerian community, I have also been involved in the successful delivery of critical projects like *Mayor of Enfield Fund Raising Committee* (2019-20) *Nigeria Uncelebrated Awards* (2016), *Nigerian Centenary Awards* (2014), *Nigerian Olympic Committee Dinner* (2012), *Nigeria at 50 Celebrations* (2010) and *African Film Festival* (then known as Afro Hollywood Awards) in 1999.

You can volunteer for a charity in your community and your professional association.

Whether you volunteer at a non-profit, charity or government body, the benefits you'll reap from doing so could have many positive effects on your future. Volunteering is important in public services is because it shows that you are committed and willing to help your community.

To volunteer is a means of giving back to society from what society has given to you. Such services can be very fulfilling because they bless your community.

4) *Join a professional association*

To fast-track your leadership development, you can also join a professional association. One of the best clubs that you can join in developing both your leadership and public speaking skills is *Toastmasters International*. You can Google it to find a local unit very close to you.

Toastmasters International, the world's premier self-improvement organisation, dedicated to improving leadership skills, self-confidence and communication through public speaking. Toastmasters International is the brainchild of an American Mid-Westerner named by Dr Ralph C. Smedley. I joined the club in 2003, and in 2005 they elected me the president of my local toastmaster club in Croydon. As the charter president of *Croydon Communicators Toastmaster*, I lead the club to win the distinguished Toastmasters Award from Toastmasters International and bagged the competent Leader Award. In 2006, I became an Advanced Toastmaster, and this involves giving advanced speeches from the communications and leadership manual over time and speak in a focused and confident way, getting the message and key points across to a variety of audience.

"In June 2010, I joined my professional association, the Chartered Institute of Personnel & Development (CIPD) South London Branch. I started out as committee member to becoming the vice chair. I am currently the chair and the 3-year tenure will be finishing this year, 2021. Also, I have just been appointed the Chair, Black on Board Community UK."

By joining the above clubs, it has helped me to develop my leadership skill.

To join a club of like minds or colleagues helps to get you connected: Iron sharpens iron. You can also expand your market by being in touch with people with whom you share the same passion and business ideas.

5) *Hang out with the right people*

As iron sharpens iron, So, a man sharpens the countenance of his friend–Proverb 27:17 (NKLV)

I love the words of Henry Ford, "*My best friends are those who bring out the best in me.*" Here is my question to you as you are reading this book right now, wherever you are in the world: who are your FRIENDS?

You can also fast-track your leadership development by hanging out with the right people.

There is this proverb in Africa that says "*Show me your friends and I will tell you who you are*".

Bob Proctor, one of my teachers, once told me: "*The people you associate with will either make or break you.*" So be careful with whom you associate and hang out with.

Dr. David McClelland of Harvard University spent twenty-five years researching success and achievement, and his conclusion was this: your reference groups, the people with whom you regularly associate, largely determine your success or failure in life. He concluded that the people you associate with daily would evaluate 90% of everything that happens to you in life. You think; walk, act, dress and talk like them, and you hold the same opinions of the people you are around most. So, associating with like-minded people is vital to making successful changes.

In the article, Dr. McClelland suggested that one should select their associations with care. In selecting your association, the people you want to be hanging out with should be people who are going where you are heading. People who add value to your life. The "Network of Enablers". In case you do not have these people in your life, start thinking of how you can attract them today. One of the best ways to attract them is by embracing the concept of professional networking.

In his book titled 'Personal Networking: How to Make Your Connections Count', Mike Cope described professional networking as "*a set of close contact or associates who will help deliver your value to the market. The key thing is that these are people who will help you in the market.*" Surround yourself with positive people who push you and make you better. Positive people who are going where you are going or those who are already where you want to be.

Michael Masterson, in his book, 'The Reluctant Entrepreneur,' described them as 'Power Network.' "*Your power network comprises all the people you know who can make a positive difference in your future. They include your mentors, consultants, competitors, vendors, colleagues, and people in high places who have resources and connections you lack,*" he said. After meeting your enablers, nurture and build the relationship with them so you can leverage it later for either your career advancement or business success.

In a report titled 'Developing Business Leaders for 2010,' which appeared in *The Conference Board*, it said that "*one of the four key essential leadership skills is relationship building/network building*".

An article in *MIT Sloan Management Review*, 'The Social Side of Performance' highlights: "*What really distinguishes high performers from the rest of the pack is their ability to maintain and leverage personal networks. The most effective knowledge workers create and tap large, diversified networks that are rich in experience and span all organisational boundaries.*"

(Source: Cross, Rob, et al. "The social side of performance: the most effective knowledge workers cultivate networks that are an optimal blend of the personal and professional." *MIT Sloan Management Review*, vol. 45, no. 1, 2003,

p. 20+. *Gale Academic OneFile*, Accessed 23 Apr. 2020.)

Renowned author Harvey Mackay says, *"If I had to name the single characteristic shared by all successful individuals, I'd say it's the ability to create and nurture a network of contacts."*

I became a strategic networker and started professionally in 2003, where things were not going the way I wanted in my business. I undertook a network analysis by listing out all the names in my telephone contact and started categorising them.

I created 5 categories, namely: *Stressors, Family, Friends, Enablers* and *Mentors*.

Surprisingly, many people fall into the Stressors category and I only have 5 people in the enabler's category and one person in the mentor's category. To be successful in life and career, you need more facilitators and mentors, and that is what I have been able to achieve today, which has impacted my life and bank balance positively.

Your network is an excellent source of leverage. When you need something you don't have, you reach out to your system to see if someone has it. Almost all successful individuals understand the power of leverage. Using leverage speeds up success in any endeavour. You may become successful without using leverage but, if you aren't using it, that means you will compromise the level of success, speed, and time necessary to get to each level. I continually leverage my contacts to accomplish what others may say is impossible. And, in using that leverage, I make sure that it is always beneficial for both sides of the equation. In a nutshell, develop your social capital and build a network of enablers.

Gone are the days of 'heroic entrepreneurship': no one can do everything all alone. You need to learn how to find people who can help you in your business. No one is an island sufficient to himself. Our lives are interconnected; our world is a complex network of relationships. No person or business can live and survive in isolation. We must build a relationship with others. You need to network with others. You need to interface, interconnect, negotiate, inter-relate, synergise, strategise, collaborate, engage, dialogue and coordinate with others to make progress and achieve your career or business your goals faster at each stage of your life. If you want to enjoy unparalleled business success in terms of market share and your net worth, you must be able to create diversified networks rich in experience and span all organisational boundaries. Start creating and nurturing a network of powerful support networks because your network determines your net worth. Expand your circle of contacts and leverage your social capital because your network determines your net worth.

6) *Look for a mentor because success leaves a clue*

"Seek direction from one who's already there." — *an Old Zulu saying*

Success leaves clues — Look for those who have done what you want to do. Identify a mentor and be coachable. Most successful people, even geniuses, have mentors to give them perspective and learn from the experience of others. Socrates mentored Plato ... Plato mentored Aristotle ... and Aristotle tutored Alexander the Great. Benjamin Graham mentored Warren Buffett ... Thomas Edison mentored Henry Ford....... and Jim Rohn mentored Tony Robbins and Les Brown. And Les Brown, Robin Seiger, Pat Utomi and Pastor Ladi Ayodeji mentored Dayo Olomu. Mrs. Duncan mentored Oprah Winfrey, and W. Clement Stone was Jack Canfield's mentor. Moses mentored Joshua ... Elijah mentored Elisha... and Jesus mentored his disciples.

Now, who are mentors? Great leaders have great mentors.

Richard Branson attributes Virgin Atlantic's success to his business mentor and aviation expert Sir Freddie Laker. Dr Martin Luther King Jr praised Benjamin Elijah Mays as his spiritual mentor. Finding the right mentor(s) is your fastest, easiest, most reliable way to master any skill. It's akin to finding the shortcut to your success! If you want your business to grow ten times in size, who better to help and guide you than someone who has already made that journey and has built a successful business or career themselves?

7 Things to look for in a mentor

1. *Empathy*

2. *Complementary Skills*

3. *Inspiration*

4. *Generosity of Spirit*

5. *A History of Success, especially someone who has been when you are aspiring to be*

6. *A Wide Range of Experiences*

7. *Someone who has overcome adversity*

You can also look for a mentor online and offline. Also, you may have a mentor in different areas of your life.

My mentor, Professor Pat Utomi, a Political Economist and Management Consultant, taught me how to balance work and family. He often tells me that *"Hard work does not kill" "Man's self-worth outweighs his net worth"* and *"What determines a man's long-term worth is his integrity and competence."*

7) *Sowing seeds that benefit others.*

Become a mentor

If you have attained a bit of success in your career or business, become a mentor or volunteer your expertise for a good cause. Pursue success with significance in mind. Do your little of good to leave this world better than you met it. Support a good cause and leave a good legacy.

"... when you get older and look back on your life; you'll ask yourself a bunch of questions. Did I make a difference? Did I contribute something? Did my being here matter? Did I do something that left an imprint? The trouble is, many people get towards the end of their lives and don't like their answers. And by then it's almost too late."

Visualise your funeral and consider what you would want friends to describe as, your legacy is an excellent way to clarify what is important to you and what you want to achieve.

Asking people to spend just a minute imagining a close friend standing up at their funeral and reflecting on their personal and professional legacy helps them to identify their long-term goals and assess the degree to which they are progressing toward making those goals a reality.

Nine minutes into his famous Stanford commencement speech, Steve Jobs discusses the importance he placed on thinking about death during life. He said, *"Remembering that I'll be dead soon is the most important tool I've ever encountered to help me make the big choices in life."*

Scientists now agree he was on to something:

Thinking about death can be a good thing. An awareness of mortality can improve physical health and help us re-prioritise our goals and values, according to a new analysis of recent scientific studies.

I started as a Black Mentor for Southwark Council in 1997, where I mentored young people to gain self-confidence and value education. Since then, I have tutored over 1,000 people who are now thriving in their career and business both in the UK and Nigeria.

8. Start a Mastermind Alliance Group

Mastermind Alliance Group, as the name implies, requires a meeting of the minds. The origins go back a long way. Ancient Greek philosophers such as Socrates enjoyed lively debate and an opportunity to share their ideas and insights. I started one with a group in 2004 called MAGPIES, which means *Mastermind Alliance Group of Professionals who model Integrity and Excellence*. It was made up of 9 people, and the primary purpose is to establish support for each other emotionally, professionally and personally. It also provided a unique forum for sharing ideas, information, and discussing meaningful topics on everyday challenges.

9. Shadowing opportunity

Job shadowing is another method to fast-track your leadership development. 'Job shadowing' is following someone around, who is doing their job. You go into the workplace and observe someone doing a job you'd like to do by shadowing them.

If you know a leader you admire who is doing what you like, you can send them an email requesting an opportunity to shadow them.

I received over ten requests of this nature yearly from up-and-coming speakers who request to shadow me while speaking at a conference.

When I started my leadership journey years ago, I have also requested for a job shadowing opportunity. In 2015, I shadowed one of the UK's most successful Black Member of Parliament when he was campaigning. I travel from London to be part of his campaigning team, and I shadowed him the way he was wooing voters. He has been their MP for over 25 years.

The most important thing is to ask, because if you don't ask, you don't get.

10. *Brand Yourself*

How can you stand out from among your competitors, focus on your abilities and positively influence your target audience? The answer lies in the concept of Personal Branding, a professional and effective way to present ourselves to others, which is another critical success factor. In these highly competitive times, people are constantly upgrading and updating their training in every field. Therefore, you need to market yourself properly to get a new contract or the job or promotion you are looking for. Your passion, personal knowledge, experience and abilities are essential, but you also need to present them as effectively as possible. You can do it by developing your brand, a mark that distinguishes you from all other people.

According to Daniel Priestley in his book, 'Key Person of Influence', "*Almost every two years you will sit down and dream up a whole new plan for what you do and how you do it. If you don't, you'll be overtaken by those who do. So, if there's no security in the job anymore and if businesses are constantly changing, where does someone go to create certainty? You go to your brand, your network, your experiences and passio*n." Hence you must design and create your brand.

Dare to Be You. A personal brand is nothing more than the public projection of your personality and skills. For you to develop an own successful brand, you need to dare to design it based on the way you want to be seen by the world rather than on what you believe others may think of you. You have the power to influence people to see you precisely the way you wish to be perceived simply by defining who you are — your strengths, values, goals and personality — and presenting these points in a compelling, persuasive manner. Dare to express yourself according to your values, strengths and unique traits. Create a great concept of who you are and present it to the circle of people and organisations with which you interact.

A good image is not enough while personal branding is not only having the right image. It's successfully showing how you can contribute as a member of a team. Whether it's at work or anywhere else, it requires investing time and talent in designing a proposal of what you offer, along with the ability to deliver it. Once you have decided what you offer — your experience, skills, and strong points — you must establish and define your goals as clearly as possible, and the strategies you will implement to make yourself known. If you have a clear vision of what you want to achieve in your professional life, designing your brand will give you the impetus you need to attain success. But you must also deliver what you promise.

According to Keith Ferrazzi with Tahl Raz in their book, 'Never Eat Alone', "If you're not distinct, you're extinct." A powerful personal brand is a great advantage in building relationships, making money and making an impact. Also, people who are known beyond the walls of their cubicle are more successful than colleagues of equal ability. They find jobs more efficiently. They rise on the corporate ladder faster. Their networks grow with little heavy lifting.

Building your brand can be a challenge, but it is possible and necessary. It is essential to be creative and proactive and to know how to distinguish between your image and your brand. Remember that your brand goes beyond superficial matters. It's an excellent opportunity to increase your potential and the recognition you receive in your community and your world.

Tom Peters, the world's leading brand when it comes to writing, speaking, or thinking about the new economy, said, *"You are a brand. You are in charge of your brand. There is no single path to success. And there is no one right way to create the brand called You. Except this: Start today. Or else."*

11. *Discipline*

This is one thing that you require to fast track your leadership development. To speed up your leadership development, you need to develop the discipline to focus on your development and the most critical task — the one that can advance your business or your career and often require an extended long-term effort.

According to Myles Munroe, in 'The Spirit of Leadership: Cultivating the Attributes That Influence Human Action' (2005): *"Any study of the characteristics of true leaders will reveal that they all exhibit strong self-discipline, usually motivated by a passion generated by a sense of purpose and vision. All leaders are 'prisoners' of the passion of their intentions. We may define discipline as voluntary standards and restrictions motivated by a desire that is greater than the alternatives. It is a self-policing. The nature of discipline is self-management, regulated by a code of conduct in keeping with a set of goals and commitments dictated by an intended result. Discipline is a series of decisions prescribed by a determined destiny."*

When I talk with top leaders, they tell me the most significant productivity challenge they face is a constant distraction. The problem is that even if those distractions qualify as work, like answering emails, checking social media, checking smartphone and making telephone calls, maybe they add little or no value. This is what Georgetown Professor Carl Newport calls "deep work" (also the title of his book on the topic, it labels most of these activities shallow work). This is low concentration work just about anyone can do. Deep work however requires intense focus and concentration. It's demanding but adds a lot of value. Newport says, but deep work will enable you to get noticed, get promoted and make a name for yourself. Deep work is one concept I have embraced, and it has worked for me. If we want to be productive, we have to stay focused on the kinds of projects that add real value to our businesses. But that's harder than ever today.

Also, discipline yourself to devise ways of using your mobile devices efficiently and effectively. Technology is supposed to make our lives easier, allowing us to do things quickly and efficiently, but if not carefully used, they can become weapons of mass distractions. Also, be careful of the vast array of devices, platforms, portals, website applications, software programmes so they don't turn to distractions. Beware of multitasking randomly on all your devices.

Beware of information overload. According to a 2010 survey by Basex, 94 percent of those questioned had, at some point, felt overwhelmed by information to the point of incapacity. The study showed, amongst other things, 30 percent of knowledge workers had no time at all for thought and reflection during their day, and 58 percent had only between 15 and 30 minutes. This is very alarming. Devise a way to filter information. Tecmark survey finds average user picks up their smartphone 221 times a day.

12. *Look after yourself*

Health is a blessing of which few appreciate the value, yet upon it, the efficiency of our mental and physical powers largely depends. Anything that lessens physical strengths debilitates the mind. Health is a gift appreciated most by those who have battled to achieve it. Eating right is essential for your health. Exercise regularly. Exercise strengthens the heart. Exercise lowers blood pressure. Exercise lower LDL cholesterol levels and raises HDL cholesterol. Exercise strengthens bones. Exercise lifts depression. Exercise relieves anxiety and stress. Exercise increases overall energy and efficiency in all areas of our lives. Exercise helps maintains desirable weight levels. It builds muscles and burns fat. The doctor recommends the moderate exercise of at least 150 minutes weekly. Go for a medical regular medical check-up at least once a year. I prefer the first Monday of the year. Have a good rest after a busy day and find time to reflect. Take your health seriously. *"No matter your dreams or goals in life, if you want to achieve them, you first must take care of the fundamentals: energy, wellness, relationships, spirit, and meaning."* - Arianna Huffington in *'Thrive'*.

**50 Leadership Quotes That I most admire

---

1. *"You manage things; you lead people."* - Rear Admiral Grace Murray Hopper.

2. *"If there is such a thing as good leadership, it is to give a good example. I have to do so for all the IKEA employees."* — Ingvar Kamprad.

3. *"Before you are a leader, success is all about growing yourself. When you become a leader, success is all about growing others."* — Jack Welch.

4. *"Sometimes, I think my most important job as a CEO is to listen to the bad news. If you don't act on it, your people will eventually stop bringing bad news to your attention, and that is the beginning of the end."* — Bill Gates.

5. *"The ability to deal with people is as purchasable as a commodity as sugar or coffee, and I will pay more for that ability than for any other thing under the sun."* — John D. Rockefeller

6. *"Never doubt that a small group of thoughtful, concerned citizens*

can change the world. Indeed, it is the only thing that ever has." — Margaret Mead.

7. *"Become the kind of leader that people would follow voluntarily; even if you had no title or position."* — Brian Tracy

8. *"Your arrows do not carry, observed the master; because they do not reach far enough spiritually."* — Zen Master

9. *"I start with the premise that the function of leadership is to produce more leaders, not more followers."* — Ralph Nader

10. *"Effective leadership is not about making speeches or being liked; results define leadership, not attributes."* — Peter Drucker

11. *"You don't lead by hitting people over the head — that's assault, not leadership."* –Dwight Eisenhower.

12. *"Men make history and not the other way around. In periods where there is no leadership, society stands still. Progress occurs when courageous, skilful leaders seize the opportunity to change things for the better."* — Harry S. Truman.

13. *"People buy into the leader before they buy into the vision."* — John Maxwell

14. *"A great leader's courage to fulfil his vision comes from passion, not position."* — John Maxwell

15. *"The challenge of leadership is to be strong, but not rude; be kind, but not weak; be bold, but not bully; be thoughtful, but not lazy; be humble, but not timid; be proud, but not arrogant; have humour but without folly."* — Jim Rohn

16. *"Outstanding leaders go out of their way to boost the self-esteem of their personnel. If people believe in themselves, it's amazing what they can accomplish."* — Sam Walton.

17. *"A true leader has the confidence to stand alone, the courage to make tough decisions, and the compassion to listen to the needs of others. He does not set out to be a leader, but becomes one by the*

equality of his actions and the integrity of his intent." — Douglas MacArthur.

18. *"Beware of those who stand aloof and greet each venture with reproof. The world would stop if things were run by men who say 'it can't be done'." —* Samuel Glover.

19. *"Leaders think and talk about the solutions. Followers think and talk about the problems." —* Brian Tracy.

20. *"Be great in little things." —* St. Francis Xavier.

21. *"A leader is one who knows the way, goes the way, and shows the way." —* John Maxwell

22. *"Great leaders are not defined by the absence of weakness, but rather by the presence of clear strengths." —* John Zenger

23. *"If your actions inspire others to dream more, learn more, do more and become more, you are a leader." —* John Quincy Adams

24. *"Cowards die many times before their death. The valiant never taste death but once." —* William Shakespeare.

25. *"Leaders aren't born; they are made. And they are made just like anything else, through hard work. And that's the price we'll have to pay to achieve that goal or any goal." —* Vince Lombardi.

26. *"If you see a snake, just kill it. Don't appoint a committee on snakes." —* Henry Ross Perot.

27. *"Great leaders are almost always great simplifiers, who can cut through argument, debate and doubt to offer a solution everybody can understand." —* Colin Powell

28. *"Leaders must be close enough to relate to others, but far enough ahead to motivate them." —* John C. Maxwell

29. *"To win one hundred battles in one hundred victories is not the ACME of skills. To subdue the enemy without fighting is the ACME of skill." —* Sun Tzu.

30. *"Be as careful as to the books you read as of the company you keep; for your habits and character will be as much influenced by the former as the latter."* — Poxton Hood.

31. *"Leadership and learning are indispensable to each other."* — John F. Kennedy

32. *"Leadership is solving problems. The day soldiers stop bringing you their problems is the day you have stopped leading them. They have either lost confidence that you can help or conclude you do not care. Either case is a failure of leadership."* — Colin Powell.

33. *"A real leader faces the music even when he doesn't like the tune."* — Arnold H. Glasgow

34. *"Effort and courage are not enough without purpose and direction."* — John F. Kennedy.

35. *"What you do has a far greater impact than what you say."* — Stephen Covey

36. *"Courage is what it takes to stand up and speak. Courage is also what it takes to sit down and listen."* — Winston Churchill.

37. *"You gain strength, courage and confidence by every experience in which you really stop to look fear in the face. You must do the thing you think you cannot do."* — Eleanor Roosevelt.

38. *"There are no working hours for leaders."* — James Cardinal Gibbons.

39. *"A good leader is a person who takes a little more than his share of the blame and a little less than his share of the credit."* — John Maxwell

40. *"Be a lifelong student, read as many books as possible."* — Nelson Mandela.

41. *"Do not fear when your enemies criticise you. Beware when they applaud."* — Ralph Waldo Emerson.

42. *"Good leadership consists of showing average people how to do the work of superior people."* — John D. Rockefeller.

43. *"When people are placed in positions slightly above what they expect, they are apt to excel."* — Richard Branson.

44. *"It takes 20 years to build a reputation and only five minutes to ruin it. If you think about that, you will do things differently."* — Warren Buffett.

45. *"I hire people brighter than me, and I get out of their way."* — Lee Iacocca.

46. *"Leadership is a potent combination of strategy and character. But if you must be without one, be without the strategy."* — Norman Schwarzkopf.

47. *"In matters of style, swim with the current; in matters of principle, stand like a rock."* — Thomas Jefferson.

48. *"Never let a problem become an excuse."* — Robert Schuller.

49. *"Leadership is the capacity to translate vision into reality."* — Warren Bennis.

50. *"Giving people self-confidence is by far the most important thing that I can do because then they will act."* — Jack Welch.

THE PREMIUM LEADER: Leadership Attributes
and Strategies for Today's Volatile World

References/
Further Readings

Abidi, S. and Joshi, M. *The VUCA company*. Jaico Publishing House. 2015.

Adair, John Eric. Action-centred leadership. New York: McGraw-Hill, 1973.

Ashimolowo, M. *35 Marks of Irrepressible Leadership: Unique qualities for unsurpassable, powerful and passionate leadership. Habits of leaders who change their world*. 2015. Riverblue Publishing. London (UK), 121 pages.

Bryant, Andrew, and Ana Lucia Kazan. Self-leadership: how to become a more successful, efficient, and effective leader from the inside out. McGraw Hill Professional, 2012.

Burns, JM. Leadership. New York: Harper and Row. 1978.

Cooper, Marc (2016), How Self-Awareness Impacts Leadership Success, Dental Practice Management, July, 19, 2016

Covey, S., McChesney, C. and Huling, J., 2012. *4 Disciplines of Execution: Achieving Your Wildly Important Goals*. Simon and Schuster.

Gilbert, D. *Adapt or be crushed by the fourth industrial revolution*. City AM. Monday 9 October 2017 7:00 am accessed Friday, 24 April 2020.

Edmondson, A. C. (2012). Teaming: How Organizations Learn,

Innovate, and Compete in the Knowledge Economy. April 2012 Jossey-Bass 352 Pages. ISBN: 978-0-787-97093-2

Fiedler, Fred (1967), A Theory of Leadership Effectiveness

Goleman, Daniel. "Leadership that gets results." Harvard business review 78.2 (2000): 4-17. Isaacson, Walter. Steve Jobs: The Exclusive Biography. 2015

Graham, Stedman (2019), Identity Leadership: To Lead Others You Must First Lead Yourself

Hansson, David Heinemeier, and Jason Fried. *ReWork: Change the Way You Work Forever*. Random House, 2010.

Jones, Tim, Dave McCormick, and Caroline Dewing, eds. Growth champions: the battle for sustained innovation leadership. John Wiley & Sons, 2012.

Laloux, F. Reinventing organizations: A guide to creating organizations inspired by the next stage in human consciousness. Nelson Parker. 2014

Luthans, F. (2005). Organizational Behaviour, New York: McGraw-Hill, Inc.

McChesney, C., Covey, S. and Huling, J., 2012. *The 4 disciplines of execution: Achieving your wildly important goals* (Vol. 34, No. 10). Simon and Schuster.

Mullins, L.J., 2007. *Management and organisational behaviour*. Pearson education.

Munroe, Myles. *The spirit of leadership: Cultivating the attributes that influence human action*. Whitaker House, 2005.

Mutizwa, Joe. *Leading Without Command: A Humane Leadership Perspective for a Vuca World*. Partridge Africa, 2015.

Northouse, Peter G. Leadership: Theory and Practice. 2015. 7th Edition. Sage Publishers. 522 pages.

O'Brien, J. and Cave, A., 2017. *The Power of Purpose: Inspire teams, engage customers, transform business.* Pearson UK.

Rohn, E. James. *The seasons of life.* Discovery Publications, 1981.

Siebert, L.A. Survivor Personality: Why Some People are Stronger. *Smarter, and More Skilful at Handling Life's Difficulties... and How You Can Be, Too.* TarcherPerigee (Penguin – USA); Revised, Updated ed. edition (6 July 2010). 256 pages. 1996

Sinek, Simon (2009). Start with Why: How Great Leaders Inspire Everyone to Take Action. New York, NY: Penguin Publishers, 2009. 246 pp. ISBN: 1591842808.

Stogdill, Ralph (1974) "Handbook of Leadership: A Survey of Theory and Research"

Tannenbaum, R. and Schmidt, W.H., 2009. *How to choose a leadership pattern.* Harvard Business Review Press.

Tanthapanichakoon, Wiroon. *The Charismatic Leader Lee Kuan Yew and the Rise of Singapore as an Asian Tiger (1st Edition): How his exceptional leadership turned Singapore into one of the wealthiest countries in the world.* Kindle Edition. 2015

The Latest Research Leadership, Harvard Business Review, April 2020

Twain, A. *Self-Awareness: How to Spot and Change Your Own Behaviour and Disempowering Beliefs With A Proven Step-By-Step Formula For Dramatically Improving Your Self ... Of Your Life* (Twain: The Emotional Series). 2014.

'What's Wrong with This Picture: Kodak's 30-year Slide into Bankruptcy.' **Knowledge@Wharton** (2012, February 01). Podcast Transcription. Retrieved from

Wong, Wilson, Stella Martorana, and Sarah Dunleavy. *The future of talent in Singapore 2030.* CIPD, 2016.

http://whatis.techtarget.com/definition/fourth-industrial-revolution Ivy Wigmore. Undated. www.whatis.techtarget.com (accessed Monday 22 March, 2021 1030 hours)

http://www.cityam.com/250741/theresa-may-sets-down-her-visiongovernment-she-slams)/.. Julian Harris. *City A. M.* online portal. Undated. (accessed Monday 22 March, 2021 1035 hours)

https://www.cityam.com/britain-needs-smart-state-not-big-government-lead-fourth/ by Alan Mak, 17 March 2017. City A. M. online portal. (accessed Monday 22 March, 2021 1045 hours)

Profile of Dayo Olomu, an agent of positive change

Dayo Olomu is a renowned human capital development expert and accomplished international inspirational speaker based in London. He is also a learning and development consultant, corporate trainer, executive coach, strategic advisor, award winning event host, best-selling author, mindfulness enthusiast and mental health champion.

He is the chair of the Chartered Institute of Personnel Development (CIPD) South London; Chair, Black-On-Board Community UK; Board Member, Southwark Diocesan Board of Education and Founder, Dayo Olomu Foundation for Leadership, Mentoring, Youth Empowerment & the Less Privileged.

Easily considered one of the most influential Africans in the UK, his call to human empowerment takes him across Europe and America as one of the world's most sought-after engagers.

Articulate and intellectually irrepressible to the point of scintillating brilliance, Olomu's uniquely engaging style has profoundly endeared him to the over 150,000 people he addresses each year on personal and professional development, achieving peak performance, wealth creation, success, motivation, networking, mentoring, management, relationship, personal success, customer service and goal-setting. His books are bestsellers amongst the African community in the UK and America.

Deploying a candid passion to his energetic and highly inspirational presentations, his compelling style has achieved a unique blend of Nigerian and British cultures, in the process presenting him as a man with a distinctively oratorical edge that accords him the unequivocal privilege of delivering his powerful messages with enthusiasm, warmth and panache.

Conscientiously justifying his own words, cast in marble, "My fulfilment is in seeing the results of my principles and strategies transforming people's lives", Olomu traverses Europe, North America, Africa and the United Arab Emirates impacting positively on professionals and businesses, and encouraging them to achieve extraordinary results, increased performance, and to profit exponentially.

An abiding passion for making a positive difference in the world; nurturing people, supporting entrepreneurs, transforming businesses, developing transformational leaders and helping clients to achieve an extraordinary result gets him out of bed every morning. His experience of interacting with people for over two decades has led him to discover that if we help people to see themselves as they can be, not as they are; then the way they think, the way they feel and the way they act will eventually be altered, resulting in achieving optimum performance.

Dr Olomu who has been mentoring Africans in the Diaspora since 1996 is listed in the first edition of UK's *Who is Who of Black*

Achievers published in 2000. He has won many accolades for his exploits on the global speaking circuit and his contributions in the African Diaspora Community.

Dayo Olomu started as a Black Mentor for Southwark Council in 1997, where he mentored young people to gain self-confidence and value education. Since then, he has mentored many people who are now thriving in their career and business.

Dayo Olomu has also turned his exemplary selfless service of enhancing professional lives into that of a philanthropist; donating his time and career in service to a less privileged society. An admirer of giving back attitude, Olomu in recognition of human responsibilities, interconnection and interrelations, volunteered and completed the *Flora London Marathon* to raise money and create awareness for Leukaemia in 2007, and in April 2008 he completed the *Flora London Marathon* again to create awareness and raise funds for *Hearts of Gold Children's Hospices*, the first children's hospice and respite care facility in Nigeria.

In March 2010, he completed the *Fleet Half Marathon* to create awareness and raise funds for *Wish for Africa* and in August 2011; he skydived to create awareness and raise funds for the *Desmond Tutu Foundation*. He also completed the *Croydon Half Marathon* in 2013 to raise funds for the homeless people in Croydon. On March 24, 2015, he took part in one of the most enduring challenges in the UK, the *100KM London 2 Brighton Challenge* to raise money to purchase wheelchairs and disability aids for disabled people in Nigeria. It took him 30 hours to complete.

During his spare time, he volunteers as a career development coach with the Shaw Trust where he provides coaching on interview skills, goal setting, self-development, confidence and motivation building to those seeking employment. He was a Business Mentor with Start-up Loan, where he mentors those who are starting in business. He is also a Key Person of Influence in the Diaspora community and has been involved in the successful delivery of critical projects like *Nigeria Uncelebrated Awards* (2016), *Nigerian Centenary Awards* (2014), *Nigerian Olympic Committee Dinner* (2012) and *Nigeria at 50 Celebrations* (2010).

He launched the Dayo Olomu Foundation in Lagos at Oriental Hotel on April 2, 2016. The vision of Dayo Olomu Foundation is to 'raise transformational leaders, mentor professionals, empower youths economically and support the less privileged in the society, especially women and children.' As at today, the Foundation has offered mentorship and support to 1500 youths, provided financial support to 100 people - mostly women, reviewed over 250 CVs and assisted 25 people to find employment and have donated soft toys and the materials to children at Heart of Gold Children's Hospices in Lagos founded by Mrs Laja Adedoyin. In the UK, Dayo Olomu Foundation (DOF), is involved in feeding the homeless people in Croydon, Surrey at The Queen's Gardens through Nightwatch charity.

The DOF is funded with proceeds from the sale of the founder's fast-selling book, *My 50 Greatest Lessons in Life & Winning Principles for Success* and support from friends. The Foundation is now partnering with a leading recruitment company in Lagos, Doheney Services Limited with a view to support some of our mentees to secure employment. On June 25, 2017, dozens of Nigerians across the UK participated in a first-ever fundraising charity birthday event in London that saw the Dayo Olomu Foundation (DOF) raised funds for two disability non-governmental organisations (NGOs).

On February 4, 2016, they honoured him with the prestigious BE (Black Enterprise) MOGUL Award 2016 at a scintillating evening event that featured and recognised the crème de la crème, and the Most Influential and Inspirational Black Entrepreneurs in Britain today.

In 2015, Olomu released his ground-breaking book, a life-transforming literary masterpiece titled, *My 50 Greatest lessons in*

Life & Winning Principles for Success. The invaluable nuggets of wisdom which are contained in this book are premised on his relationship with God, building relationships with other people and his personal development. These three core values have guided this achiever extraordinaire who was once voted one of the 10 Most Influential Nigerians in London, United Kingdom.

In March 2017, after his presentation at the biggest human resources conference in Africa, *HR Expo Africa*, they honoured him with a special plaque as a speaker.

On October 14, 2017, he received the prestigious *HeForShe Leader Award 2017 "presented to a gentleman who has met the criteria of the UN Women Solidarity Movement for Gender Equality."* He won the award for his consistent support for and empowerment of women around the world.

On October 31, 2017, he became 'Mayor of Basildon' for a couple of hours. During his brilliant presentation as Keynote Speaker at the 30th Anniversary of Basildon Black History Month, in a rare display of public amity, acceptance and affection, and in the bestowal of the highest pedigree of honour and privilege a British Mayor could ever give anyone the Mayor of Basildon walked up to Dr Olomu and placed his official chain on his neck. For the rest of his speech, Dr Olomu had the staff of the office of the Mayor of Basildon. A few hours later, he was appointed and invested with the Official Title of Distinguished Member of the Royal Biographical Institute (DM ROBIN).

In December 2017, his charity, Dayo Olomu Foundation, sponsored the Feed A Project in four states in Nigeria and donated toys to Love Home Orphanage in Lagos.

On Monday, October 28, 2018, Dayo Olomu joined big-hearted business and community leaders who pledge to sleep outdoors for one night at Lord's Cricket Ground London on Monday, October 29, 2018 to raise awareness and sponsorship from their business contacts and friends to fight homelessness and poverty in the City. They raised £80,000.

He was conferred with the prestigious award of "one of the iconic leaders creating a better world for all" by the India based, Women Economic Forum.

To celebrate in 55th birthday on 25 June 2020, he completed two marathons for Prostate Cancer UK and raised £1,250.

A holder of 160 awards in 25 categories, Dayo holds an honours degree in Business Information Systems, MSc in Human Resources and an honorary doctorate. He has a Diploma in Coaching and a post-graduate certificate in Further Education. He is also a chartered member of CIPD and a fellow of the Institute of Information Management and a member of International Leadership Association, the global network for those who study, teach, and practice leadership.

When he was appointed as a member of the Southwark Diocesan Board of Education, he received a congratulatory message from the presidency in Nigeria.

His interests outside of work are varied and include among others, running the marathon, fire walking, board-breaking, bar-bending, mountain climbing and skydiving. His long-term goal is space travel - nothing will compare to seeing the earth from space.

TESTIMONIALS/ ACCOLADES

"We had very wonderful sessions, Dr Dayo, quite resourceful and captivating. His fluid presentation has made the classes quite easier and interactive. It is indeed a successful outing" - Rt. Hon. Umar Hammed Imam, Former Speaker, Kogi State House of Assembly

"The presentation was very powerful and coherent, easy to assimilate and straight to the point" – Rt Hon. Prince M.O. Kolawole, Speaker, Kogi State House of Assembly

"The whole presentation was fantastic. The marshmallow exercise was wonderful especially what we attained from it. The strategic thinking is another one" - Elder Azamju Sheidu Tseja, Clerk of the House, Kogi State House of Assembly

"We recently invited Dayo Olomu to deliver a 1-Day corporate training in Manchester for senior executives on 'High-Performance Leadership as a Catalyst for Effective Transformation' aimed at equipping the delegates with the tools, information, principles and the strategies to become an authentic high-performance leader of the 21ˢᵗ Century. The feedback from delegates was excellent, and he got a repeat business from us. Dayo's style of training intertwines good strategies with proven examples and stories. He has a way of making learning entertaining, interactive and

fun. Dayo is a great trainer and inspires delegates to think big, start small and act now. Dayo is a real winner and highly recommended." - Eucharia Anyanwo, Conference Coordinator/Director, Skygrace Events Manchester, UK.

"I enjoyed your talk on the Power of Networking. Very inspiring." - Mr Odein Ajumogobia SAN — Nigeria's Former Minister of Foreign Affairs.

"I just wanted to say a massive thank you for your presentation. The students were revitalised after your session, and the result was a great evening of teaching and learning!" - Fiona Wheeler, Course Director CHRP, London South Bank University.

"Dayo Olomu speaks to all but speaks to one. His valuable insights resonate with you even amid several other people in the same seminar. Highly recommended!" - Shola Ajani, UK.

"Going through your profile and activities give me great joy! You are a source of inspiration for a whole generation! More grease!" - Chief Segun Odegbami (MON).

"International Centre for Development Initiatives (ICDI) the United Kingdom and our Nigeria partners, Leading Edge Academy (LEA) want to say a BIG THANK YOU to you, and express our sincere and heartfelt appreciation for the unflinching support you accorded us, for your amazing presentation and for sharing your talent and expertise with our conference delegates during the one-week event in London." - Olalekan Fadeyi, Programs & Policy Director, ICDI UK.

"Thanks for your presentation on 'Networking'. I was blown over by the whole pitch on the importance of Networking. The whole session from beginning to the end was excellent and opened my mind to the 'open' door that awaits you when you network." - Vivian Heckman, HR Practitioner.

"Thank you for your presentation on Networking for the CIPD HR Ambitions 111 to enable our members in developing their networking skills. You engaged people to start actively making professionals

relationships, which happened during the day. You showed participants how to develop and maintain those relationships in ways they understood and showed them how to maximise those relationships." - Brenda English MBA, Council Representative, CIPD South London Branch.

"Dayo took part as a speaker for the event, Les Brown's London UK tour, at Central Hall in Westminster. Dayo did a fantastic opening, his delivery as a speaker was on a level that was recognised sharing the stage with Les Brown. I received great reviews about Dayo from Les Brown and the Platinum Speakers from the US who were also at the event speaking. That is why Dayo demands the respect of all his titles, too many to mention, but as a speaker and a motivator he certainly gets my vote hands down for one of the UK's top inspirational speakers." - Herald Bradnock, CEO, Reishore Marketing UK

"Dayo did not only unknot the difficult aspect of networking at our event, but he also took our attendees through the very engaging process of practical Networking. We wish him greater attainment in many ways." - Lekan Fatodu, Publisher, Checkout Magazine, UK.

"Dayo touched everyone present in the room, even the accomplished, the confident and the self-assured. His story truly inspired us and his delivery was down to earth, light and yet powerful. On the back of his delivery, a new light has been ignited in the lives of individuals who had otherwise given up." –Demola Adesina, CEO, Testing Academy, London.

"Thank you for your valued contribution to the Black History Month event at the Clocktower complex. The audience appreciated your talk and many comments forms were filled in with encouraging words and compliments from the audience." - Krishna Ray, Ethnic Minorities Information Officer, Croydon Council, Croydon Clocktower, Katharine Street, Croydon, CR9 1ET

"This is to thank you for making Turning Point Seminar a success especially. Thank you for your life-changing presentations, which will go a long way in the history of our dear nation, Nigeria." - S.A. Paul, CEO

of Liberty Communications, Port Harcourt, Nigeria.

"I want to thank you for agreeing, at such notice, to give a brief inspirational talk to our staff. They were inspired by it, and I am particularly appreciative." - T.A. Ejueyitchie, MD Premier Records.

"I first mentored Dayo Olomu as a 15-year-old lad. Now, I enjoy his work and admire the impact he's making. He is the vintage role model I can recommend for Nigerian youths" – Pastor Ladi Ayodeji, Author & Publisher

EPILOGUE

T hank you for having the patience to read **The Premium Leader** all through to the end. I hope you have enjoyed this book as much as I did when writing it.

It has taken me about five years to put this book together; from its conception to the actual writing. I must confess that it has been an exciting, if not challenging assignment. To apply VUCA to the current world wasn't easy because of the disruptions that came in the wake of the COVID-19 Pandemic.

I have shown clearly that everyone is a leader at their individual levels. I have punctured many myths and traditional beliefs about leadership to enable you situate the responsibilities of leadership in your personal life.

The summary of my philosophy on leadership adds to the growing literature on the fascinating concept. It is my expectation that you won't just read and stop there. Indeed, reading this book is just the beginning for those who want to grow and appropriate its benefits for self-development. But the dream of all writers is to get feedbacks from the readers.

To this end, I'd like to engage you. I invite you to contact me and share your thoughts with me on your reactions to this book. Much more than that, I am available for free coaching on all the main subjects that I teach. I'd be glad to have your contact, so that you could be kept abreast of my seminal projects. Please feel free to contact me via my e-mail address and phone lines:

Dayo Olomu Publishing

Office: 0871218773

Mobile: +447956065608 (UK).

Mobile: 2348039736164 (Nigeria)

E-Mail: info@dayoolomu.com and iconicddo@gmail.com

Thank you.

I look forward to hearing from you. God bless you.

BV - #0018 - 140621 - C0 - 210/148/16 - PB - 9780955067952 - Gloss Lamination